Praise for *Business in the Cloud: What Every Business Needs to Know About Cloud Computing*

In *Business in the Cloud*, Michael Hugos and Derek Hulitzky explain the many changes that cloud computing is bringing to technology, organizations, and industry ecosystems. Their book is a tutorial written in simple language to help readers understand the potential of the cloud to transform every industry in the years ahead. *Business in the Cloud* is highly recommended for anyone who wants to take advantage of the many opportunities being brought by cloud computing to business and society.

—Irving Wladawsky-Berger
Chairman Emeritus, IBM Academy of Technology;
Strategic Advisor, Citigroup; Visiting Professor, MIT;
Visiting Professor, Imperial College

The Weather Channel is making cloud computing a cornerstone in its architecture to support severe weather events like hurricanes and nor'easter blizzards. *Business in the Cloud* is a concise but informative insight into cloud computing, is a great tutorial to quickly educate yourself (without vendor biases) on the options and capabilities of cloud computing, and should be read by all business and IT leaders responsible for their organization's infrastructure.''

—Dan Agronow
Chief Technology Officer,
The Weather Channel Interactive, Inc. (TWCi)

In today's complex business environment, flexibility and efficiency are the difference between the companies that flourish and those that perish. *Business in the Cloud* is an excellent resource to help business leaders think through the practical implications of how to best leverage the technical infrastructure required to thrive in the twenty-first century.

—Larry Bonfante
Chief Information Officer,
United States Tennis Association;
Founder, CIO Bench Coach, LLC

When a new technology platform emerges, business leaders need to understand its implications for their companies. Michael Hugos and Derek Hulitzky shift the cloud computing conversation from speeds and feeds to business opportunities and benefits. If you lead an organization that integrates business activities with technology—and today, that means everyone—this is a must-read book.

—Bernard Golden
Chief Executive Officer, HyperStratus

Whether you're currently operating in the cloud, considering moving to the cloud, or just trying to understand the meaning of cloud computing, *Business in the Cloud* explains the potential of this new model for success. A comprehensive work covering all facets to consider for the delivery of business solutions, opportunities, and customer satisfaction, *Business in the Cloud* is a must-read for all business executives tasked with leading in today's technology-mandated world.''

—Michael J. Twohig
Executive Vice President and Chief Administration Officer,
Clean Harbors Environmental Services, Inc.

Michael Hugos and Derek Hulitzky have finally given us what is missing in the swirl of all the "cloud" hype—a context. In a highly accessible manner they successfully set the stage to enable businesses to strategize and maximize the true value of cloud computing. From organizational implications, to the raw economics, to the technology itself, they provide a needed step forward and have advanced the field.

—Dr. Howard A. Rubin
Chief Executive Officer and Founder,
www.rubinworldwide.com

Business in the Cloud lays a solid foundation of the technical components that enable business growth and innovation potential in the cloud. It offers a compelling case as to why the cloud should be a part of every IT leader's strategic plan now. This book is a must-read for every business executive looking to understand how it is vital that technology align with the enterprise in our new Internet age.

—Jessica Carroll
Managing Director, Information Technologies,
United States Golf Association

Business in the Cloud delivers great insight into the genesis of cloud computing—and its business application—from two guys with their feet planted firmly on the ground."

—Enzo Micali
Executive Vice President, Technology & Operations/
Chief Information Officer, Harris Interactive

At the end of the day, the cloud computing ecosystem advances the capability for systems to work for people—rather than people working for systems. And as a technology, it is equal to—or greater than—the invention of the local area network (LAN). *Business in the Cloud* does a great job of translating the real-life thinking and effort required to adopt cloud computing—and captures the profound change potential across technology infrastructure, applications, and IT professionals.

—David Giambruno
Senior Vice President and Chief Information Officer, Revlon
2009 CTO of the Year—*InfoWorld*

Cloud computing may likely be the next foregone conclusion, driven primarily by two key forces: (1) a flexible pay-as-you-need operational cost model and (2) the growth of software-as-a-service (SaaS) solutions and application offerings. If needed improvements in security and performance monitoring come as promised, it will sway CIOs to let go of their data centers and shift to the cloud paradigm. *Business in the Cloud* provides both business leaders and IT executives with everything they need to make an informed decision on the shift to cloud computing.

—Gregory S. Smith
Chief Information Officer and author of *Straight to the Top:
Becoming a World-Class CIO* and *How to Protect Your
Children on the Internet: A Road Map for Parents and Teachers*

Business in the Cloud

Business in the Cloud

WHAT EVERY BUSINESS NEEDS
TO KNOW ABOUT CLOUD COMPUTING

Michael Hugos
Derek Hulitzky

WILEY

John Wiley & Sons, Inc.

Published by John Wiley & Sons, Inc., Hoboken, New Jersey.
Published simultaneously in Canada.

Limit of Liability/Disclaimer of Warranty: While the publisher and author have used their best efforts in preparing this book, they make no representations or warranties with respect to the accuracy or completeness of the contents of this book and specifically disclaim any implied warranties of merchantability or fitness for a particular purpose. No warranty may be created or extended by sales representatives or written sales materials. The advice and strategies contained herein may not be suitable for your situation. You should consult with a professional where appropriate. Neither the publisher nor author shall be liable for any loss of profit or any other commercial damages, including but not limited to special, incidental, consequential, or other damages.

For general information on our other products and services or for technical support, please contact our Customer Care Department within the United States at (800) 762-2974, outside the United States at (317) 572-3993 or fax (317) 572-4002.

Wiley also publishes its books in a variety of electronic formats. Some content that appears in print may not be available in electronic books. For more information about Wiley products, visit our web site at www.wiley.com.

Library of Congress Cataloging-in-Publication Data

Hugos, Michael H.
   Business in the cloud: what every business needs to know about cloud computing/
Michael H. Hugos, Derek Hulitzky.
       p. cm.
   Includes index.
     ISBN 978-0-470-61623-9 (hardback); ISBN 978-0-470-91702-2 (ebk);
ISBN 978-0-470-91703-9 (ebk); ISBN 978-0-470-91704-6 (ebk)
   1. Electronic commerce.   2. Cloud computing.   3. Web services.   I. Hulitzky,
Derek, 1961-   II. Title.
   HF5548.32.H855 2010
   004.3'6—dc22   2010023272

Printed in the United States of America

10 9 8 7 6 5 4 3 2 1

Michael Hugos: To my wife Venetia Stifler

Derek Hulitzky: To my parents and my children

Contents

Preface

The level of debate and confusion in many areas of our lives makes many things hard to see, yet also makes one thing perfectly clear. The intensity of debate and confusion are proof in themselves that big changes are under way. We have arrived at what has been variously called a "tipping point" or an "inflection point" or a "perfect storm."

Tried-and-true formulas and business models from the last 50 years no longer deliver the results they once did, and it is still far too soon to see the exact nature of the new formulas and business models that will replace them. Yet, again, this makes one thing quite clear. For the foreseeable future, organizations need to learn to thrive in environments of continuous change. Change itself will be a constant fact of our lives.

Therefore, if change is the one predictable thing in a world where so much else is so unpredictable, companies optimized to deal with change will certainly be more successful than companies not optimized to deal with change. That is why successful response to change is the new business imperative, and the practices and technologies that bring it about are the basis for sustainable prosperity in this century.

Cloud computing arises from the combination of technologies that have been developing over the last several decades. And the ongoing rapid evolution of cloud technology is driven by the pressing needs of organizations to cope with change in their markets and change in their financial situations. In a time where information and communication technology is now mission critical to every facet of business operations and where safe bets are hard to find, it is safer to explore new markets and new ventures on a pay-as-you-go basis instead of investing a large sum of money up front and hoping the investment pays off.

Cloud computing makes this possible. It can be quickly rolled out; it can be quickly scaled up to handle increased volumes if business takes off; and it can be just as quickly discontinued or scaled back to cut costs if business does not take off. This variable cost operating model allows companies to replace capital expenses with operating expenses, and that is critical to any organization operating in high-change, unpredictable environments. Cloud computing enables companies to best align operating expenses with revenue and protect their cash flow and operating profits.

In addition to its financial impact, cloud computing also affects how companies structure their organizations, how they manage and coordinate their daily operations, and how they engage and motivate their people and their business partners. In this book we explore each of these areas and show how they interact with each other. To further illustrate key points we draw on our own personal experience in business and technology and we use case studies and insights from industry thought leaders and practitioners.

This book is divided into three parts. The first two chapters provide a basis for understanding and discussing the changes we are going through. They discuss new organization structures companies are adopting and new economic realities that companies need to address. The next six chapters define cloud technology and describe strategies, tactics, and lessons learned that companies can use to adopt cloud computing and to put it to effective and profitable use. The last two chapters expand upon the information in the previous chapters and offer insights into successful business practices and operating models as well as thoughts about the global, cultural, and societal impact of cloud computing.

We have worked hard to make this book accessible to a broad audience of readers from business, technical, and academic backgrounds. As best we could, we balanced the need for a comprehensive framework to understand cloud computing and its business impact with the need for a simple and direct discussion of the key points without delving so deeply into specific details that we lose the interest of a large number of our readers. Our intention is to give you a body of knowledge and insights that enables you to engage in a thoughtful and spirited conversation with others about how to navigate the profound changes that are reshaping the way we use technology and the way we conduct business.

We would love to hear from you regarding questions, comments, or issues you have about the book and the ideas we put forth. Please feel free to contact us; our email addresses are shown below.

Michael Hugos
Chicago, IL USA
mhugos@yahoo.com

Derek Hulitzky
Milford, MA USA
dhulitzky@gmail.com

Acknowledgments

We want to thank all the people who helped us with our research and shared their insights and opinions about cloud computing and its impact on business. Some of these people are named in the text of the book and others are not, yet all of them have contributed to our thinking and the ideas we present here.

In alphabetical order, these people (and their companies when relevant) are:

Yuri Aguiar — Ogilvy Worldwide
Peter Alsberg — eCD
Mike Bogovitch — Burn the Box, Inc.
Phaedra Boinodiris — IBM
Nicholas Carr — Nicholasgcar.com
Andres Carvallo — Austin Energy
Muhammed Chaudhry — Silicon Valley Education Foundation
Willy Chiu — IBM
Alan Cohen — Cisco Systems
Ken Collier — KWC Technologies, Inc.
Pat Condon — Rackspace
Frank Enfanto — Open Sky Corporation
John Engates — Rackspace
Alan Ganek — IBM
Gene Glaudell — eCD
Bernard Golden — HyperStratus
Anthony Hill — i3Logix
Jeff Keltner — Google
Kristof Kleckner — IBM
David Knight — Cisco Systems
Ed Laczynski — LTech
Michael Martine — IBM

Tony McDonald – CSC
Steve Morlidge – Satori Partners
Srini Murti – E2open
Eric Newhuis – eCD
Jim Petrassi – CSC
Rick Pittard
Howard Rubin – Rubin Worldwide
Paul Saffo – Saffo.com
Mor Sela – Navajo Systems
Bob Sutor – IBM
Peter Tonellato – Harvard Medical School
John Treadway – Unisys
Steve Winshel – Beachbody.com
Irving Wladawsky-Berger – IWB LLC
Russ Young – LTech
Jeff Kaplan – THINKstrategies
Ken Male – TheInfoPro

CHAPTER 1

The Evolution and Future of Corporate Business Structures

In 1991, Ronald Coase won the Nobel Prize in economics after a lifetime of influence that began with the 1937 publication of his renowned paper entitled "The Nature of the Firm." In this paper, Coase asked (and then answered) the lofty question of why corporations form in a free market economy. Coase's point was simple: If there really are free and efficient markets, then a corporation can get any service it wants from a free market of independent contractors. Despite this free market, however, he cited the range of additional costs related to searching for, contracting, coordinating, and eventually paying for these services. And he showed how these costs ultimately made it more expensive to secure services in the open market versus bringing them in-house.

Coase went on to say you could measure the size of a firm by the number of contractual relations it creates, and by the number managed internally versus externally. As a result of the added expense related to external relationships, he showed how companies could then bring more and more of their contractual relationships inside in order to gain efficiencies and lower their transaction costs. This approach is what drove the creation of big, vertically integrated corporations in the twentieth century. That was the world according to Coase in 1937.

Today, a company is still motivated to bring more and more of its transactions in-house, but only until the cost savings gained are offset by other costs. Those other costs come in the form of management information overload and the resulting inefficiencies in decision making and allocation of assets.

Many companies are now bumping up against those limits. In particular, with the spread of the wireless Internet, mobile computing and business application services delivered over the Internet, it is becoming easier and less expensive to manage external contractual relationships and transactions. Instead of being optimized for internally focused inside-out communications, companies are being transformed and reoptimized for outside-in communications.

The classic hierarchical organization structure of twentieth century companies is being redesigned and this gives rise to the network organization structure of the virtual enterprise. In the virtual enterprise the activities performed internally are those that directly add value to the company's products and which its customers pay it for doing.

Irving Wladawsky-Berger is a former co-chair of the President's Information Technology Advisory Committee under Presidents Clinton and Bush, a visiting lecturer at MIT's Sloan School of Management, a strategic advisor to Fortune 100 companies, and a former IBM senior executive. He describes today's environment like this:

> Since we can now use technology, the Internet and open standards to begin to automate, standardize and integrate business processes, those transaction costs described by Ronald Coase are dropping precipitously. Consequently, the whole nature of the firm, and what it means to run an efficient business, is going through very extensive changes. These are not easy changes. Not only is there a great deal of innovation required to automate and integrate business processes, but perhaps more important, there are even greater changes in culture required to transform Industrial Age business models to something more appropriate to our Internet era.[1]

By having common standards for common transactions like purchase orders, order processing, billing, accounts payable, and so on, firms gain tremendous flexibility and they can change and adapt easily as situations evolve. Weaving technology into these transactions, and combining them with common service delivery standards, improves a company's ability to deal with a wider ecosystem of service providers. This enables companies to shift their culture and their processes so they have access to the talent and services as the need arises.

This redefines the basic culture of the firm. This notion of learning how to collaborate has become a key driver of wealth creation. Firms learn to live in their marketplace or they lose touch with their customers and cannot follow them as needs and desires change. With industrial technology the object is efficiency and low cost, with service technology the object is customer satisfaction in whatever form that may take for the markets being served.

Example of a New Corporate Organization Structure

The days of the traditional pyramid-shaped corporate hierarchy as a viable business model are coming to an end. The past 20 years have produced some winners and some losers, and some of the biggest losers are companies that built themselves into huge conglomerates that were supposed to be too big to fail. Instead they are proving the truth of the saying, "The bigger they are, the harder they fall."

It's not that companies can't be big and grow revenue to many billions of dollars. It's that they have to swear off that fatal tendency to organize themselves as hierarchical pyramids where most people are powerless drones who just follow orders while the important decisions are made by a small group of powerful executives at the top of the pyramid. Given the pace of change, companies need something more agile and responsive. As shown in Figure 1.1, an inevitable consequence of organizations using the pyramid-shaped hierarchy is that there is a decision making bottleneck at the top of the organization. No small group of executives, regardless of their smarts, hard work, or sophisticated computer systems, can make all those decisions in a timely or competent manner.

People at the top of corporate hierarchies are overwhelmed by the sheer volume of decisions they have to make; they are too far away from the scene of the action to really understand what's happening; and by the time decisions are made the actions are usually too little and too late. Companies suffer the consequences of this performance by staggering from one bad decision to another like punch-drunk boxers who can't understand what's happening and can't understand why they keep getting hit.

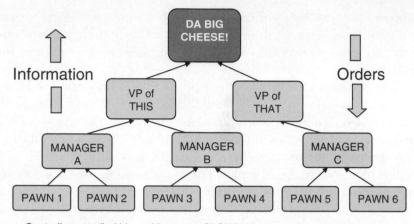

Centrally controlled hierarchies move SLOWLY because only a few people know what the strategy is and everybody else waits for permission to act.

Figure 1.1   Traditional Organization Structure

Cisco Systems got hit hard in the collapse of the dot-com bubble in 2002 when their stock went from around $77 a share to around $11. But they took that opportunity to learn some lessons that many other companies are only now starting to consider. Because human nature is what it is, it often takes a "smack-up-side-of-the-head" event to send a wake-up call and get us to consider new ideas and try out new ways of doing things.

The good news is that we really can learn from mistakes when we decide to do so. Cisco used to be a traditional pyramid-shaped corporate hierarchy where all the important decisions were made by a small group of senior executives at the top of the organization chart. Then they fell on hard times. What has emerged in the past several years is an agile enterprise with a network organization structure (see Figure 1.2) where decision making is decentralized out to some 500 managers and the whole operation is powered by Internet-based collaborative technologies like blogs and wikis and social media tools, some of which they have built themselves.

Now instead of a small group of executives telling everybody else what to do, people have authority to figure out for themselves what to do. People are motivated to coordinate, cooperate, and collaborate with each other by a financial incentive system that rewards them for their common successes instead of rewarding each manager for their individual successes.

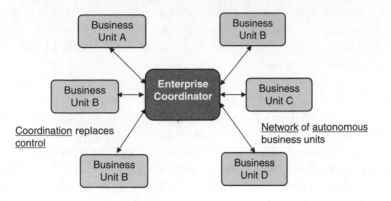

Enterprise Coordinator says WHAT. Business Units free to choose HOW.

Coordination requires everybody to know what the strategy is and have authority to act.

Figure 1.2   New Organization Structure

Cisco's CEO John Chambers makes the case that Cisco's new business model is "the best possible model for how a large, global business can operate: as a distributed idea engine where leadership emerges organically, unfettered by central command."[2] Cisco is also sharing what they've learned with big customers like AT&T, General Electric, and Procter & Gamble.

Is there a winning business model here that other companies could put to use? What kind of IT systems architecture would best support this type of business model?

Model of a Responsive Organization

The business model used by Cisco and other responsive organizations is to give their business units a high degree of autonomy in how they reach their business goals and encourage them to constantly explore their markets and look for new opportunities. The business units in these companies are organized as networks instead of hierarchies simply because network organization structures allow for greater business unit autonomy.

These companies support their network organization structure of autonomous business units by using a shared services model. In this model there is a central enterprise coordination unit that sets goals and overall strategy and provides the other business units with administrative, finance, and systems support services. This frees the business units from taking on those tasks and those expenses so they can focus on the activities that generate revenue. This also enables the company to take advantage of economies of scale in delivering these support services.[3]

As they grow, these companies keep their organizations from evolving into rigid hierarchies by following a practice of forming new business units to pursue new products and markets. Instead of letting one original business unit get larger and larger as it grows its business and enters new markets, that original business unit takes on the role of the enterprise coordinator for a host of new business units. And these new units handle the growth of existing businesses and the expansion into new markets. This is illustrated in Figure 1.3.

The evolution of corporate organization structures like this is driven by the convergence of economic necessities with technological capabilities. The need to be responsive to evolving customer needs and desires creates networks where decision making is pushed out to operating units closest to the scene of the action.

Each business unit has its own sales force and operations capability to do work. Business units get all other support services from enterprise coordination hub.

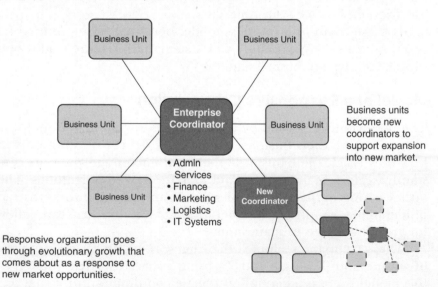

Business units become new coordinators to support expansion into new market.

Responsive organization goes through evolutionary growth that comes about as a response to new market opportunities.

Figure 1.3   Structure of Agile and Responsive Organization

And these network operating structures are supported by a mix of telecommunication and computing technologies that enable services to be delivered anywhere at any time over the Internet.

This mix of technologies and services is now known as "the cloud" or as "cloud computing." The industry research firm International Data Corporation (IDC) defines cloud computing as "Consumer and business products, services and solutions delivered and consumed in real time over the Internet."[4]

In the words of an article entitled "The Long Nimbus" published by the *Economist* magazine about the impact of cloud computing on company organization structures, "Businesses are becoming more like the technology itself: more adaptable, more interwoven and more specialized. These developments may not be new, but cloud computing will speed them up."[5]

These trends combine to produce companies and operating procedures that are much more fluid and flexible than what came before. Instead of procedures moving in a predictable straight-line fashion from start to finish (as in linear assembly lines), business processes now move in patterns that are circular and iterative and constantly adjusting to meet changing circumstances. These new processes are not industrial in nature; they are cybernetic in nature.

A Cybernetic Economy

Jeremy Rifkin is a senior lecturer at the Wharton School's Executive Education Program and has spent 10 years as an advisor to the European Union. He is president of the Foundation on Economic Trends and author of several bestselling books on the impact of scientific and technological changes on the economy, the workforce, and the environment. He is also the principal architect of the European Union's "Third Industrial Revolution" economic sustainability plan, which addresses the triple challenges of the global economic crisis, energy security, and climate change. His most recent book is *The Empathic Civilization*.[6]

In this book he states that the Internet and mobile computing and digital media are giving rise to what he calls the third industrial revolution and business models that are "cybernetic, not linear." Instead of the linear, start and stop assembly line model of the twentieth century's second industrial revolution, business is now about access to services instead of ownership of products. Business is no longer about transactions that record one-time purchases but is instead about "an ongoing commercial relationship between parties over time."[7]

Instead of purchasing music CDs, customers now buy membership in organizations that provide them with access to huge libraries of music, which they can access for their personal use. Instead of buying a car, many people are turning to membership in companies like Zipcar and iGo that provide them with the use of a car when they need one. Successful companies increasingly focus on wrapping their commodity products in blankets of value-added services that are constantly tailored to meet evolving needs and desires of specific customer segments.

Even for the most basic products, the shift toward a service orientation is evident. Take commodity products like floor wax and mops and consider this question: Do customers want floor wax and mops or do they want shiny floors? In most cases customers want shiny floors, not wax and mops. The profit opportunities and areas for business growth lie in innovative and responsive services that a company can wrap around its otherwise commodity products.

Those companies that consistently offer customers the right blend of products and services can consistently earn profits that are two to four percent higher (and sometimes more) than industry averages. This service-based additional profit can be thought of as the "agility dividend."[8] And this agility dividend is perhaps the most promising and sustainable source of profits for companies in our real-time global economy where products by themselves are so quickly commoditized.

A business model optimized for delivering this evolving mix of services to customers in an ongoing relationship over time clearly requircs a different organization structure than the traditional hierarchical structure that supported businesses optimized for selling products to customers in one-time transactions. And with any new organization structure comes the need to find new processes for control and communication in that organization structure. The centralized command and control methods that worked for hierarchies will not work for service delivery networks.

The science of cybernetics describes the control and communication processes that work best for network organizations. So familiarity with some basic principles of cybernetics is helpful in exploring how responsive network organizations operate.

Cybernetics Is about Control and Communication

The word *cybernetics* was first defined in the late 1940s for use in scientific and engineering discussions about the operations of specific systems. In the past 30 years the word has been modified by popular culture to take on meanings that were not originally intended. Cybernetics has been sensationalized and now often implies something futuristic and computerized and either very cool (as in "cyber-space") or very ominous (as in "cyborgs").

Norbert Wiener, a professor at the Massachusetts Institute of Technology, coined the term *cybernetics* in his book by the same name published in 1948.[9] He derived the word from the classical Greek term for steersman—*kybernetes*. In Wiener's words, cybernetics covers "the entire field of control and communications theory, whether in the machine or in the animal."[10]

The core of cybernetic research is the discovery that the same laws govern the control and operation of processes in any system whether that system is mechanical, electrical, biological, economic, or social. This means that the structure and workings of any process can be described and investigated using the same terms and relying upon the same principles.[11] Thus, researchers and practitioners in different fields can use a common language and build upon each other's knowledge.

Feedback Loops

Central to the understanding of cybernetics are the concepts of feedback and homeostasis (see Figure 1.4). There are two kinds of feedback: positive and negative, and both kinds of feedback operate through the use of communication feedback loops. Homeostasis means a state of equilibrium or balance. Many processes can be seen as operating to regulate or maintain a predefined equilibrium state. Let's look at each of these concepts in a bit more detail.

- *Positive feedback.* This occurs when the output of a process creates input to the process that accelerates its production of more of the same output. The effect of positive feedback is additive. It produces a result that continually builds upon itself. There is a snowballing effect. Positive feedback moves a process from one level of performance to a different level of performance. If left unchecked, positive feedback leads to the

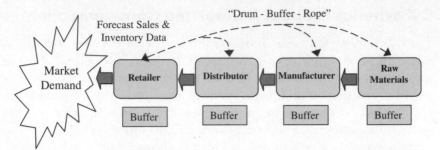

Real-time visibility of relevant data enables companies to collaborate and adjust the flow of inventory to meet fluctuating market demand.

- Market demand sets **drum** beat or tempo of supply chain.
- Manage uncertainty with **buffer** of either inventory or production capacity.
- Data is **rope** that ties supply chain together and enables self-adjusting feedback loops to operate.

Figure 1.4   Feedback Loops Drive a Real-Time Supply Chain

equivalent of an explosion or a collapse. Examples of positive feedback are a chain reaction in a nuclear reactor, a population explosion, or the growth of capital over time due to compound interest.

- *Negative feedback.* Negative feedback happens when the output of a process creates input to that process that moves the process toward a predefined goal or performance level. Negative feedback is corrective. The desired performance of a process is continually compared with its actual performance, and the resulting difference is used to take corrective action. The process adjusts its performance so as to minimize the difference between desired output and actual output. Examples of negative feedback are the operation of the cruise control in a car, which operates the car's engine to maintain a predefined speed, or the operation of a thermostat, which operates a heating unit to maintain a room's temperature at a predefined level.

- *Homeostasis.* Homeostasis is defined as the point at which the process is operating at just the right level so as to be in balance with its environment or with the expectations that have been set for it. The action of negative feedback on a process constantly moves the process toward the performance level that is defined as homeostasis. The action of positive feedback on a process can result in moving the process to a new level of performance and thus a new level of homeostasis. So, it is negative feedback that maintains homeostasis and positive feedback that changes the definition of homeostasis.

General Systems Theory

During the 1950s and 1960s, people built on the insights provided by cybernetics. At the end of the 1960s Professor Ludwig von Bertalanffy published a book entitled *General Systems Theory*[12] that pulled together and expanded upon material he had published in various articles and scientific papers over the previous 25 years. He noted that in surveying the evolution of modern science a significant fact emerges: that researchers in different fields like physics, chemistry, biology, economics, and sociology who pursued independent lines of inquiry all wound up encountering similar problems and created similar concepts to deal with these problems. The concept of a system has a rigorous definition that applies in whatever discipline or application area being discussed.

To begin with, all systems demonstrate the properties of coherence, pattern, and purpose. This means all the components of a system are interrelated in some discernable and coherent way. These interrelationships form recognizable patterns that give structure to a system. And the workings of a system are not random; it acts in a purposeful way to accomplish a goal or set of goals.

Systems are also self-regulating and persistent. Disturbances to a system from its environment will trigger interactions between the components of the system enabling it to recover from the effects of the disturbance and regain a state of equilibrium or homeostasis. This is what allows a system to persist over time in a changing environment.

Profit Potential of Self-Adjusting Feedback Loops

In an agile and responsive organization, business processes and business units must manage themselves as much as possible and not rely on centralized command and control systems. Cybernetics and General Systems Theory show us ways to design these processes. By using information flows and negative feedback loops, a company can design and implement processes that continuously correct business unit behavior in order to steer the company toward predefined performance targets. In this way, self-managing processes amplify the productivity of the company's employees.

The self-adjusting feedback loop is a very useful phenomenon. If feedback loops can be harnessed to drive business processes as efficiently as we have learned they can to drive mechanical and electrical processes, then companies can achieve whole new levels of productivity and profitability.

At present, the operating processes of most companies are rigid and inflexible. They are set for a certain way of doing things and they do not change even when those ways of doing things are no longer delivering the results that people want. Processes change only under great pressure and then they settle into a new but still rigid mode of operations that will in turn have to be changed again, under great pressure, when they no longer deliver the results that people want.

If cybernetic feedback loops were harnessed to drive business operations, then those operations would become much more flexible and fluid. Cybernetic processes are continuously adjusting to changing circumstances. Instead of waiting for a business process to drift far off course as conditions change, feedback loops can continuously adjust and reshape a business process to respond effectively as situations evolve. Cybernetics involves a mix of positive and negative feedback loops that are employed as needed to keep a business process aligned with the needs and desires of the people they serve.

Negative feedback occurs when a system compares its current state with a desired state (or goal) and takes corrective action to move it in a direction that will minimize the difference between its present state and its desired state. A continuous stream of negative feedback guides a system through a changing environment toward its goal. Negative feedback continually corrects and improves an existing process.

Positive feedback occurs when a new action or process or product generates a desirable response so the system is induced to do more of what produced the positive feedback. Positive feedback creates new processes and new systemic capabilities that did not exist before. Positive feedback creates change. It moves a system to a new position of homeostasis: a new state of equilibrium.

Computers are best used to automate the routine and repetitious activities that make up the bulk of most business operations.

Computers are good at harnessing negative feedback loops to continually adjust and improve existing operations and locate exceptions to business rules. Computers monitor massive amounts of data in real time and don't miss details, and they can scale up quickly to process enormous volumes of data as business volumes grow.

People are best used to do the creative and problem-solving activities. People are good at harnessing positive feedback loops to create new things and new processes to produce those new things. These are the activities that don't have clear right or wrong answers. These are the activities that call for people to collaborate with each other and share information and try out different approaches to see which ones work best. People are good at these activities and they like doing them, so they learn and keep getting better over time as they gain more experience.

The spread of cloud computing and near universal real time access to computing power and data is creating an opportunity to leverage the power of self-adjusting cybernetic feedback loops across entire companies and entire trading networks and value chains. Real-time data sharing and close coordination between companies can be employed to deliver continuous operating adjustments that result in steady cost savings over time (negative feedback) as well as the delivery of timely new products and services that result in significant new revenue (positive feedback).

The effect of these continuous adjustments and enhancements to business operations can generate a steady stream of savings and new revenues that may sometimes seem insignificant from one month to the next, but as years go by, they become analogous to the growth of capital over time due to the humble but powerful effects of compound interest. The profits generated this way can be thought of as the agility dividend.

How can the power of the self-adjusting feedback loop be brought to bear in a business process such as a supply chain in such a way as to generate an agility dividend? One way to do this is the transparent use of performance-based bonuses. People do what they are incentivized to do. If companies provide people with clear performance targets and timely data that shows them if they are moving toward or away from their performance targets and allows them to see the effects of their actions, then a feedback loop comes into existence.

Companies are starting to use systems that provide web-based performance dashboards to display performance data for their internal operations and performance data for their suppliers. These dashboard displays are generated in real time or near real time by business intelligence (BI) and business process management (BPM) systems that monitor data flowing inside companies and between companies.

When companies set desired performance targets, BI and BPM systems allow companies to monitor actual performance and constantly adjust operations to move closer to desired performance. These continuous operating adjustments generate quantifiable benefits and business profits that can then be used to reward people for the effort needed to achieve these targets. The availability of real-time performance data plus people's desire to receive rewards is what brings the self-adjusting feedback loop into being.

When people's interactions with each other are cast in the form of a game whose object is to achieve a set of predefined performance targets, the resulting real-time feedback loops will strongly influence people's behavior. If companies and people in a supply chain or any other business process have real-time access to the data they need, then they will steer toward their targets. If they are rewarded when they achieve their targets, then they will learn to hit these targets more often. The profit potential of the self-adjusting cybernetic business model is now unleashed. This concept is illustrated in Figure 1.5.

Viable Systems Model: A Framework for Business Agility

Stafford Beer explored the application of cybernetic principles to business and its effect on the design of business organizations. He was a cybernetic theorist, a professor at the Manchester Business School in the United Kingdom, and consulted with companies and national governments on applications of his cybernetic theories. He is widely recognized as the founder of management cybernetics, which he defined as, "the science of effective organization."[13] He synthesized many of his ideas into what is known as the viable systems model.

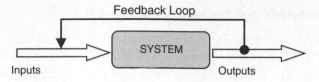

Information about the outputs that result from system actions is sent back to the system as inputs.

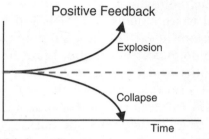

If the feedback induces the system to continue producing more of the same output, that is positive feedback.

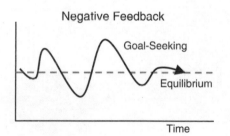

If the feedback induces the system to counteract the previous output so as to seek equilibrium, that is negative feedback.

Figure 1.5   The Power of Real-Time Visibility

The viable systems model looks at a company as if it is a living thing and describes how it should be structured to operate most effectively in its environment. Stafford Beer published two books— *Brain of the Firm* and *The Heart of Enterprise*—that explain the viable systems model[14] and provide examples of how to put it to use to achieve agility.

Model for an Agile and Responsive Organization

The viable systems model views any situation as being composed of three parts: (1) the environment; (2) the operations performed by an organization in this environment; and (3) the metasystem activities of coordination, planning, and goal setting created by the organization. This is illustrated in Figure 1.6.

Next, the model identifies five subsystems that make up the operations and the metasystem of any viable system. These subsystems are referred to as Systems 1, 2, 3, 4, and 5 (see Figure 1.7). Let's take a closer look at each of these subsystems.

System 5 is analogous to our higher brain functions. It defines the system's identity and its overall vision or reason for being. This system decides on operating policies and guidelines that the whole organization will follow and, from an information technology (IT) perspective, is supported by business intelligence and simulation systems.

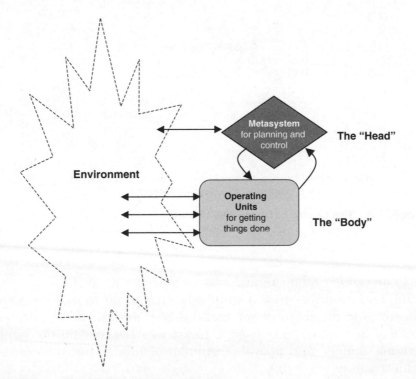

Figure 1.6   The Viable Systems Model

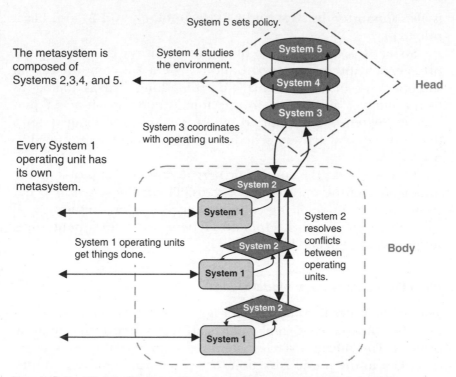

Figure 1.7   Viable Systems Model—Subsystems 1, 2, 3, 4, and 5

System 4 is like our conscious nervous system. It looks out at the environment, collects information, and makes predictions and forecasts about the environment. It also picks strategies and makes plans for best adapting to the environment. IT systems that support these operations are systems like BI and simulation modeling. System 4 functions are also supported by technologies known as complex event processing (CEP) systems. CEP systems filter through multiple data streams emanating from other systems looking for predefined patterns or sequences of data that would indicate situations of interest to the organization.

System 3 is the system that looks across the entire body of muscles and organs and optimizes their collective operations for the benefit of the whole body. This system also performs functions that are analogous to those of the autonomic nervous system. In addition, System 3 is responsible for finding ways to generate synergies between operating units. From an IT perspective this operation is also supported by BPM and CEP technology, and BI also has a role to play.

System 1 is the collection of operating units that carry out the primary activities of the organization. System 1 is composed of all the operating units that actually do something. This is analogous to the muscles and organs in the human body. From an IT perspective System 1 is supported by transaction processing systems like order entry, delivery scheduling, and customer relationship management.

System 2 is like the autonomic nervous system that monitors the interactions of the muscles and organs. This is the system that has responsibility for resolving conflicts between operating units and for maintaining stability. From an IT perspective this operation is supported by BPM and CEP systems.

What the Viable Systems Model Means

The model states that in order for a system to be a viable system it must be able to create, implement, and regulate its own operating policies. This means a viable system needs to have the five systems described in the previous section. If a system cannot create, implement, and regulate its own policies then it is a component part of some other system because such a system all by itself would not have the ability to sustain itself over time.

It also emphasizes that the individual operating units (the System 1s of an organization) need to be as autonomous as possible. They need to be free to devise and execute their own operations within predefined performance ranges and areas of responsibility. Each System 1 operating unit is actually a microcosm of the entire system. Each operating unit contains its own Systems 1 through 5. In other words, the viable systems model is a fractal organization; it is a set of repeating components and processes that manifest themselves at lower and lower levels of detail within the organization.

Because each System 1 operating unit is autonomous and self-regulating (this is what makes agility possible), their activities are not directly controlled by Systems 2 and 3 but instead they are co-ordinated through the action of feedback that occurs between Systems 1, 2, and 3. Systems 2 and 3 monitor data generated by System 1 and look for changes in status or for indications that an operating unit has gone outside of agreed-upon operating parameters. BPM technology is designed to perform these monitoring tasks.

When a status change or an out-of-range condition is detected, Systems 2 and 3 send this information back to System 1. This sets up either a positive or negative feedback loop that guides the activities of the individual operating units and brings them back into line. Response by an operating unit to feedback from System 2 or 3 allows it to regulate its own behavior and respond as needed. (This is what it means to be agile.)

Response to feedback should not be confused with just following an order. System 2 or 3 does not order System 1 to do something. Instead, the guiding effect produced by feedback between these systems is an alternative to centralized command and control. This enables each System 1 operating unit to act autonomously. And this autonomy allows each unit to think and act on its own as long as it stays within agreed-upon limits. The viable system as a whole then benefits from the initiative and responsiveness displayed by the autonomous operating units. As well, Systems 2 and 3 are not bogged down trying to do the thinking for System 1, so they do a better job of monitoring, coordinating, and maximizing overall system performance.

A Cloud-Based Model for Business Organizations

The metasystem functions that Stafford Beer described are very similar to the functions performed by the enterprise coordinator in the model of a responsive organization discussed at the beginning of this chapter. If we merge these two models and put the metasystem and coordination functions in a cloud-based technology environment, we get a model of what cloud-based business networks could soon look like.

It makes sense to place the metasystem and coordination functions in the cloud because these are collaborative activities and the cloud is a highly effective platform for collaboration between different companies. Business intelligence and simulation systems in the cloud can provide all the companies in the network with transparency and visibility so they can all see the real-time status of network operations. Cloud-based simulation modeling systems can then provide all companies in the network with a common collaborative platform for testing out new operating processes.

Decision makers from the different organizations in the network can then engage in a fact-based collaborative decision-making process. A process called simulation gaming can be used to evaluate the effectiveness of different decisions. These simulations will show the most probable results of different decisions so that it becomes clear which decisions will best advance their common interests. The simulation gaming process is immersive and inclusive and those qualities will tend to generate consensus among the decision makers. (We'll later discuss this application of what is known as "serious games" in Chapter 10.)

It also makes sense to put the communication and coordination functions in the cloud because that provides companies with a common data transport and communication system in which they can all connect. Cloud-based systems have well-defined application program interfaces (APIs) so each company can use service-oriented architecture (SOA) techniques to connect their internal systems to a cloud communications backbone. This is illustrated in Figure 1.8.

Will cloud-based systems built with BPM, CEP, BI, and simulation gaming come together as cloud-based management and governance models for entire industries? This could be the formation of integrated sets of real-time workflow processes that are tailored to specific vertical industries. And these systems could evolve over time to embody field-tested libraries of industry best practices that enable highly responsive and profitable business processes in specific vertical markets.

Cloud-based trading networks like this would then enable the formation of entire business ecosystems. They could, in effect, become the equivalent of global industry operating systems. As these industry operating systems take shape, they could evolve as open source or proprietary operating systems. Will a single company own the operating system or will larger groups of companies own the operating system in common? It's way too early to tell.

Companies may be more inclined to join networks where they have some ownership and greater influence in the decision-making procedures employed by the network. On the other hand, proprietary operating systems may be more efficient and faster to react to changes because fewer people are involved in the decision-making process. Ultimately, the dynamics of these two models could turn map to those of centrally planned economies versus free market economies.

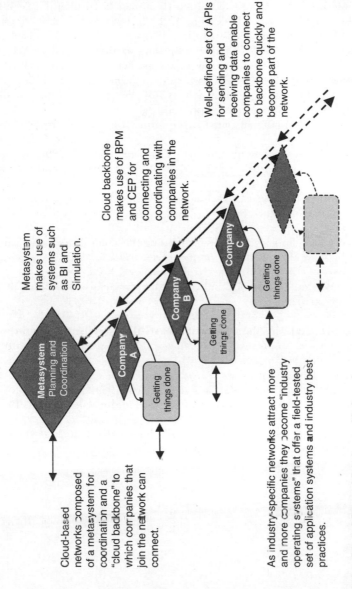

Metasystem makes use of systems such as BI and Simulation.

Cloud backbone makes use of BPM and CEP for connecting and coordinating with companies in the network.

Well-defined set of APIs for sending and receiving data enable companies to connect to backbone quickly and become part of the network.

Metasystem
Planning and Coordination

Company A

Company B

Company C

Getting things done

Getting things done

Getting things done

Cloud-based networks composed of a metasystem for coordination and a "cloud backbone" to which companies that join the network can connect.

As industry-specific networks attract more and more companies they become "industry operating systems" that offer a field-tested set of application systems and industry best practices.

Figure 1.8   Cloud-Based Business Network

Notes

1. Irving Wladawsky-Berger, "The 'Outside-In' Enterprise," October 10, 2005, blog post http://irvingwb.typepad.com/blog/2005/10/the_outsidein_e.html.
2. Ellen McGirt, "How Cisco's CEO John Chambers Is Turning the Tech Giant Socialist," *Fast Company*, December 1, 2008, www.fastcompany.com/magazine/131/revolution-in-san-jose.html.
3. Thomas Hoffman, "From Cloud Computing to Shared Services: Why CIOs Are Taking a New Look at Sharing IT Infrastructure and Applications," *CIO* magazine, September 2009, www.cio.com/article/500629/From_Cloud_Computing_to_Shared_Services_Why_CIOs_Are_Taking_a_New_Look_at_Sharing_IT_Infrastructure_and_Applications.
4. Frank Gens, International Data Corporation (IDC), 2009, http://blogs.idc.com/ie/?p=422.
5. Ludwig Siegele, "The Long Nimbus," *Economist*, October 2008, www.economist.com/research/articlesbysubject/displaystory.cfm?subjectid=348909&story_id=E1_TNQTTRGQ.
6. Jeremy Rifkin, *The Empathic Civilization: The Race to Global Consciousness in a World in Crisis* (New York: Jeremy P. Tarcher/Penguin, 2009).
7. Ibid., p. 538.
8. Business and technology practices for earning the agility dividend are explored in the book by Michael Hugos, *Business Agility: Sustainable Prosperity in a Relentlessly Competitive World* (Hoboken, NJ: John Wiley & Sons, 2009).
9. Norbert Wiener, *Cybernetics* (Cambridge, MA: Massachusetts Institute of Technology Press, 1948).
10. Ibid., p. 11.
11. A book that examines the impact of cybernetics on society is also written by Norbert Wiener, *The Human Use of Human Beings: Cybernetics and Society* (Boston: Houghton Mifflin, 1950).
12. Ludwig von Bertalanffy, *General System Theory: Foundations, Development, Applications, Revised Edition* (New York: George Brazillier, 1969).
13. Stafford Beer, *The Heart of Enterprise* (New York: John Wiley & Sons, 1979), p. 372.
14. Stafford Beer, *Brain of the Firm* (New York: John Wiley & Sons, 1981) and *The Heart of Enterprise* (New York: John Wiley & Sons, 1979).

CHAPTER

2

The New Economics of Business

Volatility is here to stay. Scaling operations up and down smoothly as conditions change and the ability to pivot quickly and address new threats or opportunities are what make companies successful in today's economy. Business models with high fixed costs are much riskier than they used to be. What happens if actual demand for a company's products is less than predictions? Can the company still be profitable and cover operating costs if only 60 percent of its capacity is utilized? What if only 40 percent of its capacity is activated? Companies with high fixed cost investments in unused production capacity are risking their profits and their very existence.

In the twentieth century, businesses around the world learned the lessons of industrial efficiency and economies of scale. Given reasonably reliable predictions of customer demand and stable prices for labor and raw materials, companies were able to make large capital investments in plant and equipment to achieve economies of scale and meet demand for their products at the lowest per-unit costs, and thus earn the greatest profits. They paid for these investments and their resulting high fixed costs through increases in productivity that enabled them to produce greater and greater amounts of standard goods and services at lower and lower costs.

This was the basic business operating model for most of the twentieth century. But now market volatility is increasing. Products have life cycles measured in months or a couple of years at most. Technology and consumer preferences are rapidly evolving. New fashions and new products and whole product categories pop up without warning, drastically altering traditional customer buying patterns. Not only is product demand hard to estimate, but so too are the costs of everything from raw materials to labor and transportation. The real-time global economy of the twenty-first century is a very different world from that of the last century.

In volatile times, responsiveness trumps efficiency. It is a better business strategy to trade fixed costs for variable costs. Even though operating costs will rise as business activity rises, costs will also drop as activity drops and costs won't rise at all if expected activity levels don't materialize or a new product doesn't take off. The responsive business model is better for companies wanting greater ability to manage their cash flows and protect their operating profits. This variable cost model is less risky. Although companies can't maximize profits as efficiently as with a high fixed cost operating model, a responsive model gives companies the flexibility to adapt to change and opportunities as quickly as they happen.

Moving to a Variable Cost Operating Model

If we define variable costs as those costs that can be readily scaled up or scaled down in 90 days or less, what percentage of total company operating costs can be considered variable? A lot of companies are faced with high fixed operating costs because of capital investments in plant, equipment, and other assets that cannot be easily reconfigured or quickly sold off. When economic conditions don't match expectations, companies find themselves in the difficult position of having to apply drastic measures to reduce their costs.

Drastic measures take a toll on companies. Repeated downsizing of staff leaves remaining staff demoralized and worried about their own future. Spinning off and selling company business units can reduce operating costs, but the hurried nature of these sales often results in less-than-favorable prices. And some assets simply can't be sold because they are so specialized to unique company operation— or because, over time, they have become obsolete and their value is negligible even though their related operating costs continue to rise.

Companies Need to Operate in Unpredictable and High-Change Markets

If they absolutely have to, most companies could reduce operating costs by 25 to 30 percent over a year through drastic measures and much grief. But this approach isn't something that can be repeated often or it will destroy the very fabric of the company. This means these companies can operate over the long term only in markets where product demand and prices don't vary more than 5 to 15 percent from one year to the next; essentially, that's the extent they can vary their operating expenses without destroying themselves. These kinds of markets were common 50 years ago. How many markets like that still exist? Which way is the trend going?

What if companies could easily achieve operating expense reductions or ramp up expenses to support production increases without tearing themselves apart in the process? What if a company had an operating model where half or more of its operating costs were variable costs? This kind of company could survive and even thrive in much more volatile markets. And this kind of company would be much better suited for business conditions in this century.

Companies optimized for the more predictable industrial world of the twentieth century are like race cars that achieve great speeds and win races—as long as the course is straight and flat. But when the course makes sharp turns and winds through landscapes of hills and valleys, speed alone no longer wins races. In this century, winning cars and winning companies need to be maneuverable and responsive; they need to shift from a focus on speed to a focus on agility. This is illustrated in Figure 2.1.

The Merging of Business Operations and Information Technology

There was a time not so long ago when all the technology needed to operate most businesses was a phone, a fax, a pen, and paper. Computer systems were mostly used to support back office administrative operations and weren't part of front office customer-facing activities or daily operations. Now, the phone itself is a computer, faxing is one of many services handled by computers, and pen and paper have been displaced by digital communications. Businesses from new start-ups to global corporations now depend on computer systems that thread through everything they do, every hour of every day, front office and back office. Most daily business activities are supported by real-time systems, and operations would come to a halt if their supporting systems stopped.

Companies can't launch new products or services or redesign internal operations without new application systems to support them. In fact, the cost and time involved in developing new systems

Which race car do you want to drive on the "economic race course" of this century?

Race Car A—speeds up to 200 mph on the straightaway; sharp turns cause car to crash; slow parachute-assisted deceleration

Race Car B—speeds up to 150 mph on the straightaway; capable of sharp turns; can decelerate quickly

"Economic race-course"

20th Century Industrial Economy

21st Century Real-Time Economy

Figure 2.1   Economic Racecourse of This Century

was often the reason companies didn't want to roll out new products or redesign the way they ran their operations. It was just too expensive and too much trouble to do new things, so they perpetuated old products and continued with old ways.

Recent studies show that information technology (IT), the business application systems it supports, and the data centers and staff needed to run the technology and systems, average about six percent of business operating expenses.[1] Yet, ironically, IT and systems are a critical factor in any company's ability to be agile and responsive. This six percent of the operations budget has critical leverage over the profitability of the business as a whole if it can be used to deliver better business responsiveness and agility. More ironic is that, at present, about 70 to 80 percent of company IT budgets goes to the operation and maintenance of existing systems and data centers.[2] So in many organizations, there isn't much money available to design and develop new systems.

Is there a way for companies to shift the expense and complexity of IT operations that are not part of a company's core competencies to outside vendors? Can vendors who specialize in those operations deliver higher levels of service at lower cost because of their expertise and economies of scale? Could companies then shift the bulk of their IT spending to developing new systems to support continuous evolution and modernizing of existing products? To introduce brand new products? Would this give companies the agility they need and a better return on the 94 percent of their operating budgets they dedicate to non-IT operations and product delivery? Would this enable companies to transform themselves into the maneuverable and agile race cars best suited for the twenty-first century economy?

Information Technology Finally Becomes a Utility

A historical analogy sheds some light on what is happening today. Consider the development of the modern city and the buildings and utility services that made the modern city possible. A little more than 100 years ago in Chicago, the world saw the birth of the modern-day skyscraper. Many architects were drawn to Chicago in the years following the Great Chicago Fire of 1871 because it destroyed the growing city's central core and created an open landscape. The city had a pressing need for new development that created great opportunities for talented architects and builders who could meet the challenge. Architect William Le Baron Jenney designed the first load-bearing steel-frame building that became the 10 story Chicago headquarters of the Home Insurance Building completed in 1885. In the years that followed, the steel-frame skyscraper became the symbol of the modern city.

People who worked in those buildings, and the buildings themselves, depended on a steady and reliable supply of electricity to support their operations. For the first several decades after the skyscrapers were built, they relied on electric power generators installed in their basements. Fueled by coal, these massive mechanical devices required constant care. Mechanical engineers and electricians were required on staff to make sure that the business conducted in these prestigious buildings was not interrupted by the lack of power. These buildings were created to be self-sufficient.

At the same time that the steel-frame skyscrapers were being built, another innovation was changing how companies operated. Chicago businessman Samuel Insull, who had earlier been one of the founders of the General Electric Company, presided over the creation and growth of the Commonwealth Edison Company. Insull's electrical power company grew steadily and he leveraged its increasing economies of scale to deliver reliable electric power at lower and lower rates to acquire more and more customers.

The Move to Public Power Grids

During the 1910s, companies that owned and operated skyscrapers began considering outside vendors to supply their electricity and debated whether or not it made sense to tap into the new, emerging power grids. From one perspective, building owners saw advantages in getting rid of those expensive electricity generators in the basement. No more coal deliveries, no more staff to shovel the coal day-in and day-out. No more mechanical and electrical engineers on staff. But from another viewpoint, there were just as many people concerned about whether a new power grid would be reliable. Why should we take the chance on a new power grid, they argued, when the building was already self-sufficient?

The finance and accounting people pointed out that electric utilities were able to deliver electricity at lower and lower costs per kilowatt hour compared to the in-house electric power generators.[3] The in-house electric power people countered that relying on outside utilities was a performance and security risk. How could one know if the outside electric utilities would always deliver reliable power? And how could one know if they would stay in business? And then there was the big security question: Since outside electric power would come to the building through exposed electric cables, what if someone cut the power lines to the building? How could they guarantee the security of outside power supplies?

These were all valid concerns, but not enduring reasons to maintain power generation within individual buildings. Electric utilities steadily became more reliable and it became clear they wouldn't go out of business. Power security issues were addressed, and maintaining power reliability and minimizing interruption became an appropriately important area of the power industry's focus.

By the 1920s, the debate about whether to rely on in-house power generation or to outsource that function to an electric power utility was over, and we all know who won that argument. In the end, it wasn't really so much about "who" as "what." The bottom line won the debate. The idea of providing ongoing, nonemergency, day-to-day power for a skyscraper from an independent provider isn't even a discussion, let alone a debate, today. When it comes to a contest between security and productivity, the winner is always productivity (except in a small number of isolated and clearly defined situations).

As the twentieth century progressed, companies no longer carried the fixed costs associated with generating their own electricity. Whether they were early power grid adopters or were laggards, companies and building owners eventually tapped into the public power grid delivered by electric utilities. And they redirected the money they once spent on generating power to activities that created a much better return on their investment.

Fast-Forward 100 Years

Now, as we debate the pros and cons of outsourcing computing functions to computing utilities, the arguments and concerns are in many cases similar to the electric power debate a century ago. Just substitute computing power for electrical power and the analogy is complete. Why should a given company maintain a large data center, along with the staff and resources to operate it? On the other hand, why would a company trust its data center operations to a service provider? The concept continues to be argued in many circles. IT vendors stand at the ready and heavily promote their utility computing or cloud computing capabilities (and some organizations consume them on a substantial scale). At the same time, there's an entire landscape of corporate IT organizations concerned about this model who debate the challenges related to service-level agreements, outages, data security, and more.

It comes down to a basic question that each company must answer: "What business are we really in?" If companies don't have to worry about all of the financial and operational overhead associated with building and operating their own data centers, would they then be able to focus more on what they do as a business? As recession era budgets continue to stagnate, and CFOs constantly question capital expenditures, companies are increasingly challenged to investigate and then make use of more efficient ways to deploy basic computing power. How companies and their in-house IT groups structure themselves—and what activities they chose to focus on—will be critical as more outside service providers are able to deliver 1) reliable computing power at 2) cost-effective price points based on 3) their increasing economies of scale.

Variable Cost IT Operations Enable Business Agility

The biggest technology opportunity for companies today is to reduce their total expenses through targeted IT investments that are converted from sunk capital models to variable cost operating models. In this high-change and unpredictable economy, many business leaders have drawn the conclusion that they must steadily move to a variable cost operating model if they are going to thrive.

Dr. Howard Rubin, a researcher in techno-business strategy and global software economics, is Professor Emeritus of Computer Science at Hunter College of the City University of New York.[4] He's done extensive research on the potential impact of companies moving to cloud computing models. His data clearly shows companies have to adopt a variable cost operating model through skillful use of IT in order to enable business agility and thrive in the next few years.

Dr. Rubin observes that IT is still a young, emerging field with only about 50 years of history to date. He suggests that the real impact of IT is only now starting to reveal itself. According to Dr. Rubin, "I'm like Darwin in the Galapagos Islands. I collect data, look at patterns that emerge and try to figure out what they mean." Then he described some patterns from his research and described what they might mean.

The Patterns Reveal an Interesting Story

Dr. Rubin's research shows that, as a whole, company revenues and company operating expenses for the U.S. economy converged in 2008, wiping out profit margins. As a result, companies started to look for ways to reduce operating expenses. Since IT is a large part of the operating expense in most companies, business leaders have naturally focused on reducing IT expenses. Dr. Rubin observes that, "Technology spending has collided with current economic conditions as IT organizations have failed to enact agile IT economics and make their value proposition transparent. The pressure is on to cut IT."

But he goes on to say that there's a big difference between cutting costs and optimizing costs, and that a lot of companies are confusing the two concepts. Companies often lump all IT expenditures into a business overhead category when, in reality, much of their IT expenditures are for growing revenue and reducing operating expenses. As a result, a good portion of IT expense is not really overhead.

Dr. Rubin's research reveals that IT financial models in most companies have only a 30 to 35 percent variable cost. The rest of the IT budget is fixed cost composed of capital expense related to the cost of purchasing IT infrastructure, and the fixed cost of people to run that infrastructure. Traditional cost-cutting strategies involve cutting staff, renegotiating vendor contracts, and delaying new projects, but the cumulative effect of these actions isn't really that much. Instead, Dr. Rubin's research suggests, companies would be far better off if they lowered the fixed cost of their IT infrastructure.

The data goes on to show that there's big opportunity to reduce IT costs by reducing unused IT infrastructure capacity through use of Dr. Rubin's concept of the "IT Commons" that could provide companies with a 60 percent or more variability in their IT operating expenses, resulting in money that could then be spent on proactively developing new, contemporary systems instead of backward investment in maintaining legacy systems.

Optimize, Resize, and Give It Up

The IT Commons is being created right now by companies like Amazon, Google, Hewlett-Packard, IBM, Microsoft, and other IT vendors who are building out enormous data centers and offering their computing power and software applications on a pay-as-you-go basis. These organizations offering pricing based on economies of scale that will ultimately drive down the total cost of IT services.

Dr. Rubin explains that the opportunity of the IT Commons concept is for companies to leverage the computing marketplace and to take advantage of rapid commoditization of IT services for nonstrategic business functions like running data centers and standard applications like email, human resource information systems (HRIS), enterprise resource planning (ERP), customer relationship management (CRM), and so on. "Give it up," he said, "if a provider can do it better and more efficiently, then go with them." In addition, he advises companies to engage in transformational IT sourcing activities like server virtualization, virtual desktops, cloud computing, and software-as-a-service (SaaS).

Companies engaged in these transformational IT activities that leverage the resulting economies of scale to reduce IT operating expenses will see total IT spending go down as a percentage of revenue go down, even though IT spending as a percentage of total company operating expenses goes up. This is the difference between optimizing IT spending and simply cutting IT costs. Ultimately, companies that understand how to optimize their IT spending will achieve more agile business models. Companies that don't understand this concept will experience the difficulties inherent in clinging to outmoded, traditional behaviors during times of rapid change.

Desirable Characteristics of the New IT Architecture

In the current economy, companies are looking for ways to cut IT expenses, yet the real opportunity is to find ways to manage total *company* expenses so that they track with the demands of business operations. Saving 10 or 20 percent on a company's IT budget is relatively small compared to deploying IT wisely to save 10 percent on the company's overall operating expenses—or by using IT to grow company revenue by 10 percent.

With newer technologies, companies have the opportunity to shift from the traditional fixed cost IT operating model shown in Figure 2.2 and move toward a variable cost model like that shown in Figure 2.3. Companies can power their business operations with IT infrastructure that meets three operating standards:

1. Low capital expense
2. Variable cost of operations
3. Scalable computing platform

Lower capital expenses are the order of the day because revenue and profits are under intense pressure, credit markets are tight, and loans are harder to get. So there is naturally less money for capital investments. As well, since we're experiencing a period of rapid technological change, big capital investments in technology are risky

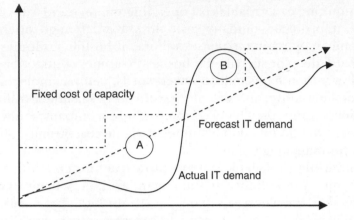

In the traditional IT operating model, the cost of IT capacity is fixed and only roughly corresponds to actual demand. Often there is oversupply of capacity, as shown by A and sometimes there is undersupply of capacity, as shown by B.

Figure 2.2   Traditional Fixed Cost IT Model

and might result in owning technology that becomes obsolete much faster than expected. So smart executives are finding ways to get systems in place without a lot of up-front capital expense. They're learning to shift their investments from building wholly owned data centers to delivering new business operating capabilities.

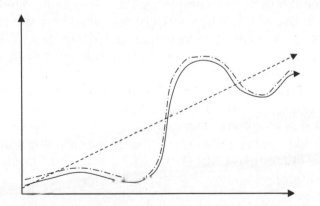

In the variable cost IT operating model companies can closely match IT capacity with actual demand and thus link IT expenses with company activity and revenue.

Figure 2.3   New Variable Cost IT Model

Committing to a variable cost operating model standard is smart because it protects company cash flow. Pay-as-you-go operating models mean operating expenses will rise if business volumes rise, but will also drop or stay small if business volumes contract or grow more slowly than expected. In other words, you pay more only if you're making more, and you pay less if you're making less. In our increasingly unpredictable economy where companies need to experiment to find new opportunities, variable cost business models are best for managing financial risk.

Committing to scalable systems infrastructure enables companies to enjoy the benefits of these standards. A scalable systems infrastructure enables a company to "think big, start small, and deliver quickly." Company executives can create strategies with big potential and try them out quickly on a small scale to see if they justify further investment. Companies can quickly start by targeting 80 percent solutions that address the most important technology requirements first, and then build additional features and add more capacity as business needs dictate and revenue climbs.

A Combination of Technologies Creates Cloud Computing

Since the turn of this century, several different, but related, types of information technology have been rapidly evolving and are now collapsing together to deliver computing resources on demand almost anywhere in the world. When technologies involving the Internet, web browsers, virtualized servers, parallel computing, and open source software are combined, they produce an entirely fresh set of possibilities for delivering computing resources.

The term *cloud computing* is the concise description of these combined technologies. IT vendors are offering the resulting package to companies that want to outsource some or all of their traditional IT operations like running data centers and operating traditional application packages like ERP, HRIS, CRM, and other business support applications.

Some Working Definitions of Cloud Computing

The exact definition of cloud computing is still evolving. Different IT vendors put their own spin on the definitions they offer, but there is increasingly more agreement than difference in their definitions. Here are several working definitions:

- "A style of computing where scalable and elastic IT capabilities are provided as a service to multiple customers using Internet technologies."[5]
- "Consumer and business products, services and solutions delivered and consumed in real time over the Internet."[6]
- " . . . a broad array of web-based services aimed at allowing users to obtain a wide range of functional capabilities on a 'pay-as-you-go' basis that previously required tremendous hardware/software investments and professional skills to acquire."[7]
- " . . . a way of utilizing resources wherever they may be when you need to use them. In that sense you just need to insure that your networking, security, and hardware infrastructure are robust enough to deliver the resources when needed, but just as important, your applications need to be able to execute well in that environment. To me it is having what you want, when you want, through your virtual desktop no matter where you are."[8]

From these three definitions more (just do a web search on "cloud computing definition") we can easily see there are three particular characteristics widely agreed upon that describe cloud computing:

1. *Practically unlimited computing resources.* Resources like computing power, data storage space, and additional user sign-on IDs for applications are available on demand as needed and this enables a high degree of agility and scalability in meeting evolving business needs.
2. *No long-term commitments.* Computing resources are immediately available and they may be used as long as needed and then retired because they are acquired on a month-to-month or even a minute-to-minute basis.
3. *Pay-as-you-go cost structure.* Because there are no long-term commitments, the cost of cloud computing resources is a variable cost, not a fixed cost; cost fluctuates depending on the amount of usage.

Cloud Computing Has Three Component Layers

Cloud computing technologies continue to change rapidly. Certain components are changing so fast that the names, and technical details of how they operate, change significantly every 6 to 12 months. Nonetheless, we can still group cloud computing technologies in three basic categories or layers. These layers support each other, and the relationships between the layers (and the way each of the layers operates) remain relatively stable. We'll use these three layers to create a basic model of cloud computing and provide a framework to discuss cloud computing technology (see Figure 2.4). These three layers are:

1. Hardware virtualization
2. Data storage and database management
3. Applications and application development environments

Not that many years ago, companies deployed applications on a dedicated server or sets of servers. This resulted in some servers

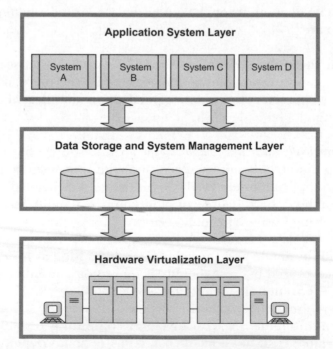

Figure 2.4   Three Technology Layers of Cloud Computing

remaining idle or running at less than full capacity at any given point in the day or the business cycle. Today, *hardware virtualization* refers to the abstraction of physical computer resources so that many different computers or application servers appear to be available to run different application systems even though there may be a much smaller number of physical servers in the environment. The term *virtual machine* (VM) refers to a software implementation of a computer or application server that executes programs like a real physical machine, but that server is tapping the resources across a pool of virtualized servers in order to maximize efficiency. As a result, hardware virtualization enables companies to optimize the use of physical computer resources and improve system administration. Virtualization is a common practice on mainframes and is becoming widely available for other computer architectures like application servers built from low-cost computer chips and commodity hardware. In the cloud computing world, this layer is also referred to as *infrastructure-as-a-service (IaaS)*.

Data storage and database management in virtualized hardware environments is far more efficient and flexible than ever. Instead of buying a new physical server to host each different database, those different databases can be supported by different virtual machines. The processing power of these virtual machines and the storage capacity of these databases can then be dynamically changed based on actual business requirements on demand and as they occur. In addition, these different virtual servers can be set up to run different operating systems like Linux or Windows as needed. In the cloud computing world, this layer is also referred to as *platform-as-a-service (PaaS)*.

Applications and application development environments can leverage hardware virtualization and data storage and database management capabilities in a cloud computing environment. Application systems to support different business operations can be hosted on virtual machines that are scaled up or scaled down hour by hour and as needed to meet changing business user demands. In this environment, new copies of a given application system can be created instantly and put into operation as needed. In cloud computing, this layer is referred to as *software-as-a-service (SaaS)*.

Depending on what system developers wish to use, application systems can be developed on cloud computing platforms that support different programming languages, testing platforms, and system management tools. Some popular development environments are provided by Google and Amazon and Microsoft. Popular programming languages that are supported include languages like Java, PHP, Ruby on Rails, and C#. (In Chapter 3, we'll explore more of the different kinds of technology that are used in each of these three cloud computing layers.)

Implications of the Transition to Cloud Computing

Momentum created by the pressures of our present economy is driving us to more widespread implementation of cloud computing. Larger companies are creating their own internal "private" clouds, and smaller companies are moving to clouds from external service providers commonly called "public clouds." The twin concerns of performance and security are valid as companies transition to these models, but they are increasingly met with practical conversation and decision making, rather than just excuses or reasons to avoid a switch to cloud computing. Vendors are rapidly delivering tools to respond to and manage these concerns.

The move to cloud computing is the most profound evolution, if not revolution, since the emergence of the Internet. It is challenging (if not causing) significant change to the ongoing mission of in-house, corporate IT groups—and especially to the way they are run. In its traditional model, the bulk of staff in these departments has been devoted to IT functions including operating and maintaining data centers, data networks and PCs, as well as the monitoring and enhancing of application systems that are hosted in those data centers or running on desktop PCs. Continued adoption of cloud computing will shift most of these traditional activities out of corporate IT groups and into the cloud service provider organizations.

In fact, the information technology profession as we have known it for the last several decades is dying; its obituary is already written. Companies are transferring the risk of high-ticket technology investments—like wholly owned data centers and internal application hosting—to highly focused and specialized service providers. Who's looking after the network? A service provider. Who's monitoring application performance? A service provider.

Because of cloud computing, in-house IT professionals in most organizations are facing big changes in their careers, what they do, and their earning power. The spread of cloud computing is, quite simply, disrupting the enterprise. Just as some IT professionals in the 1980s resisted introduction of PCs in their companies, and some IT professionals questioned the value of the Internet in the early 1990s, some IT professionals are now resisting the introduction of cloud computing in their companies. As in previous, disruptive eras, new technologies reduce demand for certain traditional skills and they change the way the IT profession is organized. Cloud computing is no different.

Cloud Performance and Security Concerns

Just as performance and security were central to the debate 100 years ago about whether to rely on outside vendors to provide electric power, they remain central to today's debate about cloud computing. Not surprisingly, there are many technology vendors creating products to address these performance and security concerns.

New start-ups and established IT vendor companies are developing performance monitoring tools for cloud computing environments. Cloud computing service providers are buying these products to support the growth of their cloud computing businesses, and to assure their customers that they can monitor performance and consistently deliver high levels of service. For many application systems, there are adequate performance management tools already available. In other cases, there are still significant technical issues to be addressed. But if the history of technical development in the past several decades is a guide, we'll see continued and rapid technology progress address these issues.

IT vendor companies are increasingly rolling out suites of new products to address security for cloud computing environments including tools that deal with cloud intrusion prevention and global threat correlation. By using these products, companies can create computing and collaboration environments that integrate their in-house IT infrastructure with cloud-based application systems, and they can exercise a high degree of control over who enters those environments and what information those people can access.

As these products rapidly improve, they're analogous to good brakes on a race car; the better the brakes, the faster you can drive the car on the winding roads of the twenty-first century. Good performance monitoring and security protection enable companies to go faster and faster in deploying new cloud computing applications because they eliminate the worry about performance and security that would otherwise slow them down. (We'll go into more detail about performance monitoring and cloud security in Chapter 4.)

Cloud Computing Drives the Creation of New Businesses

Under the relentless pressure of economic necessity and unpredictable market conditions, companies have to find ways to shift the cost and risk of basic IT operations to outside vendors. These vendors are already amassing huge demand for their services and are making the investments in data centers that create economies of scale that enable lower price points. Cloud computing data centers are evolving into the factories that supply computing power, data storage, and application systems that can drive improved margin and efficiency in the rest of the global economy.

Plans to simply cut IT budgets and to try to keep operating expenses down until business rebounds won't work. If companies restrict IT operations and IT is seen and used by their company simply as a cost center instead of a strategic thread through the collective needles that make up the company's value proposition, then the company won't be able to roll out new products in a timely manner, or keep up with changing needs of its customers, or respond quickly enough to new threats and opportunities.

Hanging onto internal IT infrastructure may prove to be a losing and precipitously risky strategy, much like it was when electric power naysayers avoided the public power grid 100 years ago. Instead, a far better move will be to find ways to enable the transition to the cloud, and to move your company to a more variable cost operating model. This creates opportunities for business leaders to show their companies how to move to cloud computing along with the ways to effectively address the related performance and security concerns. When companies make this move, they will free up money and resources to invest in more of the things their customers pay them for, and they'll create the evolving stream of products that keep them connected to and relevant to their customers. This, after all, is what history proves that earns consistent profits.

This shifting of functionality to outside service providers needs to take place so that in-house IT groups can redirect their time and money to working with the business units. They need to help the business units create real customer value with technology. All of this is similar to how social media are fast becoming another way companies spread the word about their products—and is challenging the consumption of traditional media. IT as customer support and relationship management is how modern companies need to connect with their customers and build long-term relationships. Information technology is now woven throughout so many products—like financial services, consumer electronics, smart phones, Internet applications, entertainment, and consumer services—that companies need to offload all of the routine parts of technology management so they can focus more on how to weave the technology in their products. It's simply a matter of competitive survival. Companies that apply their resources to the products that better integrate technology will win a higher share of consumers and business.

Universal access to low-priced electric power made possible by the spread of electric utilities drove a wave of innovation not only in how businesses operated but also in the products they developed. From the 1920s onward, the introduction of thousands of new products using technologies like electric motors and vacuum tubes became possible because dependable electric power became ubiquitous. As a result, how many new companies were created to build and sell products built with components like electric motors and vacuum tubes and transistors? And today, what business innovations and new products can you imagine will be created based on universal access to low-priced cloud computing power? How many new companies will be created to develop and deliver those products? We're in an era of new opportunity enabled by cloud computing.

Notes

1. Dr. Rubin, "Technology Economics and the Current Economic Crisis," Slide Presentation, slide number 10, 6 February 2009, Chicago, Society of Information Management Executive CIO Roundtable.
2. The itmWEB Site™, IT Budget Allocations Benchmarks, www.itmweb.com/blbenchall.htm.
3. This topic has been provocatively covered by Nicholas Carr, *The Big Switch* (New York: W.W. Norton & Company, 2009).
4. Dr. Howard Rubin, Rubin World Wide, New York, www.rubinworldwide.com/rubinww.php.
5. Darryl Plummer, "Experts Define Cloud Computing: Can we Get a Little Definition in our Definitions?" Gartner Blog Network, January 27, 2009,

http://blogs.gartner.com/daryl_plummer/2009/01/27/experts-define-cloud-computing-can-we-get-a-little-definition-in-our-definitions/.

6. Frank Gens, " Defining "Cloud Services"–an IDC update," IDC Exchange, September 30, 2009, http://blogs.idc.com/ie/?p=422.

7. Jeff Kaplan, "Simplifying the Term 'Cloud Computing,'" Datamation.com Blog, June 25, 2009, http://itmanagement.earthweb.com/netsys/article.php/3826921/Simplifying-the-Term-Cloud-Computing.htm.

8. Frank Enfanto, VP of Worldwide IT Operations, ACI Worldwide, private email correspondence with authors, December 22, 2009.

CHAPTER

3

Key Technologies Used in Cloud Computing

The "cloud" in the term *cloud computing* is a metaphor for computing resources (hardware and software) that companies and users access without the need to know exactly where that hardware and software is physically located. It is also used as a graphical symbol for the Internet in diagrams of computer networks to depict the varied technology infrastructures the cloud conceals. The cloud graphic has been quite common over the decades. "Despite its recent surge in popularity, the cloud is among the oldest pieces of computer jargon," according to Alex Bochannek, a curator at the Computer History Museum in Mountain View, California. For decades engineers drew them in schematic diagrams to show where their own network joins another whose inner workings are unknown or irrelevant. "You symbolize that with a cloud, or some amorphous shape," says Mr. Bochannek.[1]

Despite the vague symbols used by engineers, the combination of growing and widespread availability of broadband Internet access along with use of the Internet to deliver computing services has enabled elaborate cloud computing models to become a reality. Unlike previous eras in computing, today, the Internet and web browsers now easily connect disparate hardware and software resources that often sit well beyond the physical borders of companies. By sharing resources with other customers, the allure becomes the potential for lowered cost of using the resources for all customers. The attractiveness of this arrangement among adopters is why

International Data Corporation (IDC) predicts that IT spending on cloud IT services will be $44.2 billion in 2013—a significant rise from an already substantial $17.3 billion in 2009.[2]

Cloud Computing Defined

Today's cloud computing services provide common business applications online that are accessed from a web browser, while more traditional computing models of the 1960s through the 1990s involved users accessing software resident on a computer owned by the company or (after the introduction of the personal computer) on the very computer they were using.

Hardware and software companies—whether they sold large mainframe computers, personal computers, or any size in between—made their basic living with this model. Today, some companies still sell software licenses to companies for multiple users to access a software package, but that business model is challenged by the attractiveness of the cloud computing model.

The cloud computing concept has evolved well beyond just software delivery. Today, it's widely accepted that cloud computing comes in three major forms:

1. *Software-as-a-service (SaaS)*, whereby a software provider delivers and hosts an application, without the need for the customer to house and maintain the application in its own data center.
2. *Platform-as-a-service (PaaS)*, which is a development environment where a customer can create and develop applications on a provider's computing environment, thereby eliminating the need to find company-owned infrastructure for the development.
3. *Infrastructure-as-a-service (IaaS)*, which allows companies to essentially rent a data center environment without the need and worry to create and maintain the same data center footprint in their own company.

Forces Driving Adoption of Cloud Computing

Adoption of these key forms of cloud computing has gained momentum, largely the result of three major evolutionary forces. The first of these forces is the fact that widespread availability of the

Internet has allowed software companies to distribute their products and services (along with updates) with a mouse click and a credit card rather than through the traditional packaged software model. This has inherently changed the way in which the software is not only delivered, but updated and monitored through the software company's own computers.

The second evolutionary force is driven by innovative software companies that have pushed the delivery envelope even further. For example, Salesforce.com, largely known for its suite of contact management products designed to organize prospects for a customer's sales department, has become a pioneer in a model that hosts not only the application for a company on Salesforce.com's computers, but also the customer's data. Use of Salesforce.com has become widespread, and it has become a model in the software industry for delivering software applications with cloud computing, or in this case, what's called "software-as-a-service" or SaaS as it is popularly abbreviated. Adoption of the SaaS model has paved the way for other solution providers to sell more than just software. Today, vendors are actively positioning their offerings to also include IaaS (primarily as data centers and storage) and PaaS (elaborate software development environments housed by a vendor that don't require a company to purchase the entire environment, but to share it with others).

The third evolutionary force has emerged as large, computing intensive companies (such as Amazon.com, Hewlett-Packard, Google, IBM, and Microsoft) that have vast data centers to manage the global demand for their offerings, find themselves in a position to allow other companies to use their computing power. In fact, they now sell time and space on their computers—in what they call infrastructure-as-a-service—to other organizations willing to use it as a utility.

The concept is nothing new. As early as the 1960s, computer timeshare services were selling excess capacity on mainframe computers. What's different about today's model, however, is the scale, speed, and volume at which excess capacity can be delivered to many companies from one data center. Microsoft has also emerged as a key player with its Azure development environment it calls an operating system-as-a-service. Azure is a place where developers can build and manage applications without concern about the infrastructure limitations within their own,

Cloud Computing

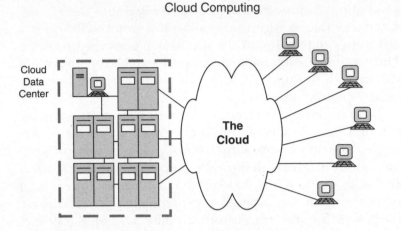

Cloud Computing—combination of applications, computing power, and data storage as a metered service with low initial cost to acquire and pay-as-you-go operating model

Figure 3.1   Cloud Computing

company-owned environments. Even Salesforce.com, widely recognized for its customer relationship management (CRM) software, is now positioning its broader Force.com development environment, infrastructure services, and social media platforms as more diverse cloud computing options that capitalize on markets well beyond the sales automation tools at the core of its historical business.

"Cloud computing is a reincarnation of the computing utility of the 1960s but is substantially more flexible and larger scale than the [systems] of the past," says Google executive and Internet guru Vint Cerf. The ability of virtualization and management software to shift computing capacity from one place to another, he says, "is one of the things that makes cloud computing so attractive."[3] See Figure 3.1 for an overview of cloud computing.

Cloud Computing Still Has Many Issues to Address

All of this said, many questions remain about cloud computing, particularly among CIOs and their teams who are target customers, and who are ultimately responsible for the particular business problems it might solve. Security, reliability, standards, and service-level agreements top the list of their concerns. MIT's *Technology Review* says, "As a still-maturing technology . . . cloud computing has yet to overcome certain challenges, such as guaranteeing the integrity and security of users' data, providing a seamless user experience, and establishing standards to allow companies to move from provider to provider."[4]

In addition, outages tend to make for good news and when a company's data is unavailable for a short period, it's often a show of the fits and starts the emerging cloud industry will experience until reliability is better perfected. Innovation, however, will prevail, as maturity of the model continues, and as CIOs and their teams learn to balance risk versus reward.

Software-as-a-Service

The leading, early driver of more widespread adoption of cloud computing has been the software-as-a-service (SaaS) delivery model. With this model, a software provider licenses its software application to be used and purchased on demand over the Internet, rather than as a prepurchased site license housed on internally maintained hardware and software infrastructure. As more computers and companies began to access the Internet, the SaaS model became more and more viable compared to the traditional software model of purchasing site licenses, or packaged software for every user. Moreover, it eased the process of downloading updated applications, renewing and disabling software as necessary, and other administrative functions.

There are many reasons this model has become more popular and more widely adopted:

- More than ever before, knowledge workers and consumers have more access to computers and to the Internet, thereby increasing their ability to access software when it is available as a service.
- Early in the era of Internet expansion (from the mid-1990s to 2000), there was corporate reluctance to conduct mission-critical business over the Internet because of reliability and security. Today, those concerns have faded as the Internet has developed a very strong backbone for secure commerce.
- Network speeds continue to improve, thereby minimizing application response times (known as latency) for users.

- Mainframes and traditional software licenses—traditionally a significant expense for companies to maintain—have become a target for cost reduction, along with the cost to maintain space for them, as well as the salaries and benefits provided to the in-house staff to operate and enhance them.
- Over the decades, web-based interfaces have enabled applications to become more standardized and easier to understand and use, so the user base of software applications has become more savvy and willing to use them.
- With basic software platforms in place and available as a service, many independent software vendors have emerged that will customize applications even further for a specific vertical application, industry, or market. Since the applications are web-based, those customized versions are now more easily marketed and distributed to even more customers in the same market, regardless of their global location.
- Small and medium-sized businesses have shown an appetite for purchasing software-as-a-service applications like enterprise resource planning (ERP) or CRM or supply chain management that previously were available only in traditional delivery models and affordable only to the largest of corporations.

Also fueling adoption is the increased sophistication with which applications are being built by providers. As a provider acquires more customers for its applications, it can increase the complexity of how it hosts those applications in order to make them more efficient for the entire customer base.

At the most basic level, the provider gives a single customer its own, customized version of the application and runs the application on the provider's servers.

The next level of sophistication is when the provider has configured the application such that many customers can use the same application (using the same application code on the provider's servers), while at the same time, allowing individual customers to customize and configure the application based on their specific needs. The advantages to the provider with this model are significant since the provider then focuses on maintaining a centralized code base.

Even more efficient is the configurable, multitenant model whereby the provider has hosted the application for many customers so that one instance of the software serves the entire customer base. This allows for the provider to maximize the use of its available server resources.

The most sophisticated model adds scalability to all of the above scenarios. Simply by organizing its software architecture to do so, the provider can make it easy to add or decrease servers to its hosting environment to meet the demands of increasing amounts of customers, or to match peaks and valleys in daily demand for the applications. This provides for an efficient use of all the provider's computing resources.

Along with the pioneering Salesforce.com, some emerging players in software-as-a-service delivery include: Google Apps, which allows any user (consumer or enterprise) to manage Microsoft Office–like files at no charge on Google's servers; 37signals, which provides companies with basic business and collaboration applications such as project management and contact management; and Zoho, a provider of various business applications that can be purchased a la carte.

Server Virtualization

The conversion of traditional computing environments to what is called a virtualized environment has also accelerated the movement to cloud computing. Simply put, virtualizing a computing environment means that the various hardware and software resources are viewed and managed as a pool, and organized so that users and applications can use that pool more efficiently than before.

Many parts of a computing environment can be virtualized, including servers, operating systems, storage, networks, and desktop computers. In all cases, the objectives of virtualization are to centralize management and to scale and use the available computing capacity as efficiently as possible among the users and applications.

For example, operating systems can be set up to run as multiple, virtualized images and to run simultaneously in order to maximize efficiency. Networks can be virtualized so that available bandwidth can be partitioned into separate channels, thereby reducing network complexity and improving the ability to manage the overall network. Storage virtualization allows pooling of many storage resources so that all available storage is assigned and managed centrally. Similarly, server virtualization allows computing power across many servers to be pooled and managed for better efficiency. Finally, desktop virtualization allows organizations to deploy less expensive desktop devices that instead place the computing power centrally in a virtualized computing environment.

Only a few years ago, most computer servers were implemented to run a single operating system and a single application. For example, an accounts payable system, or a human resources information system, or a customer relationship management system would each sit on its own dedicated server to be accessed by the appropriate employees in the organization. While this made sense in order to allocate computing power to dedicated applications, and because some applications used different operating systems that had to be installed on those dedicated servers, it also meant that those same servers were underutilized during times when the applications weren't being used as much, or at all. Multiple studies show that, on average, most servers are used to only 20 percent of their total capacity.

Software advances have changed that. Today, by adding a relatively thin software layer—a hypervisor—that enables virtualization, the multitude of servers in an organization can be pooled so that the computing power across them can be shared and allocated as needed by each individual application. In more specific terms, the software environment of a company can be organized so that many "virtual machines" (VMs) can operate on just one physical server. In these cases, the individual applications think they have access to a dedicated processor, network, and storage drive, but the hypervisor is really controlling the resource the applications need. This provides CIOs and their teams with more agility and flexibility as they can now bring up and reallocate new applications quickly and without the previous burdens of configuring individual servers for them.

Organizations have quickly found ways to apply virtualized environments to consolidate the number of servers they need to operate, and to maximize the efficiency of the applications and servers they operate. For large data centers, the implications are immense. See Figure 3.2 for an overview of server virtualization.

Nonetheless, virtualization has only scratched the surface of opportunity. According to Gartner in October 2009, 18 percent of workloads were on virtual servers. That said, Gartner expects that number to jump to almost 50 percent by 2012, impacted substantially by small and medium-sized businesses that are now taking advantage of lower price points.[5]

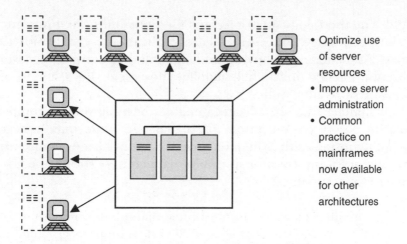

• Optimize use of server resources
• Improve server administration
• Common practice on mainframes now available for other architectures

Server Virtualization—is the partitioning of some smaller number of physical servers into larger numbers of virtual servers that each has the appearance and capabilities as if it were running on its own dedicated physical machine.

Figure 3.2   Server Virtualization

Up until then, large enterprises were almost exclusively fueling demand for virtualized environments as they saw more immediate benefits of—and could justify the expenditure to realize—server consolidation and savings on power, cooling, and server floor space.

Virtualization has enabled cloud computing solution providers to deliver dramatic economies of scale in their environments, thereby enabling a more cost-effective way for companies to compute across the cloud provider's resources. In addition, the adoption of virtualization technology has been the single largest driver of what's called a *private cloud*—a term used to describe how many CIOs are now organizing their internal data centers and related technology infrastructure.

In a private cloud, hundreds of servers and storage devices are connected to form a virtualized infrastructure. In this case, the software applications used by the company's employees aren't permanently assigned to specific servers or storage devices. In this kind of data center environment, the virtualization software allocates when and where computing and storage resources are needed across these hundreds of devices. CIOs with large data centers particularly like this methodology since it assigns the right computing resources to the peak usage times of specific applications, and avoids the sprawl associated with buying and maintaining servers that were previously needed only to help manage those peak times, and would otherwise sit relatively idle.

Efficiencies that virtualization enables have significant implications on power consumption, particularly in large data centers. According to Kenneth Brill, Executive Director of the Uptime Institute, the billowing costs of sprawling data centers should be a big concern for companies:

> The number of servers in the United States has grown from 5 million in 2000, to 10 million in 2005, to a projected 15 million in 2010. More servers eat up more electricity and energy costs go up. To avoid future energy shortages caused by increasing IT demands, 10 more power plants need to be built to the tune of $2 billion to $6 billion each and their cost is ultimately going to get passed on to IT through increased utility bills. If we are going to install an additional 5 million servers before 2010, senior IT executives had better understand the true cost of server ownership in order to make the right investment decisions. IT power consumption is going up so rapidly that data centers, which used to cost $20 million to build, now can cost $100 million—and some are in the $500 million range, excluding hardware and network costs.[6]

Ultimately, while virtualization offers an opportunity to consolidate servers and curb data center growth and power consumption, the real promise of cloud computing is in providing companies with an opportunity to avoid new data center build-outs in the first place. The very idea of expanding data center capacity by turning it over to a cloud service provider is the potential economic opportunity for both the provider and the company that needs data center resources.

Service-Oriented Architecture

The advent of service-oriented architecture (SOA) has accelerated development of the software components used in cloud computing. SOA is an architectural philosophy and is based on the idea of organizing software code so that one set of data—and the code written to process it—can be reused by other applications in the organization, thereby creating a highly efficient environment. In these cases, the data and code written to be reused is called a service (years ago a similar concept involving reusable blocks of program code was called a subroutine). In this environment, sanctioned services can then be made available on various platforms and across networks, thus maximizing their availability for reuse among various constituents, developers, and users across the enterprise.

A simple example of this reuse of a service is when an organization captures all the names and contact information for its customers in a single database. One software developer in the organization may have a need to access several pieces of that contact information to enable functions for the sales organization. That developer will write software code to access the data for that particular application.

At the same time, another developer in the organization may have a need to access the same data in order to invoice those same customers. If the code is written with a service-oriented philosophy, it would be packaged as a service, and any developer in the organization could then reuse that code (or service). The result is a net reduction in the amount of time and redundancy in the organization's development time.

SOA initiatives are typically championed by the organization's chief enterprise architect, a software professional given the substantial responsibility to organize the organization's software development efforts with consistency, standards, and efficiency. Naturally, SOA has become a key philosophical component of the role of today's enterprise architect and the software environments they manage. See Figure 3.3 for an overview of SOA software.

Web-oriented architecture (WOA) is a term used to convey a similar concept, and has emerged as a way to describe how service orientation in software development is applied to applications that are designed to be delivered over the Internet.

SOA is an attractive approach to CIOs and, specifically, their enterprise architects because it can help organizations quickly make changes to existing applications, or create new applications, as their markets change and their business needs to adjust in a more agile fashion. In addition, it can simplify how a company accesses some of the legacy systems and databases that were created prior to adoption of SOA approaches. Overall, the concept of SOA

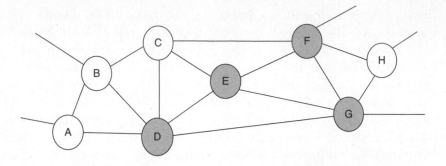

Service-Oriented Architecture (SOA)—is a style of systems architecture that combines loosely coupled services to support requirements of business processes and users. Software services on a network (network could be within data center or across Internet) can be combined as needed in support of evolving business processes. Could also call this **web-oriented architecture (WOA).**

Figure 3.3   Service-Oriented Architecture for Software

helps enterprise architects, and the software leadership in a user organization, to bring clarity to how the company organizes its applications and software infrastructure.

SOA requires a commitment, though. From one point of view, executive leadership needs to encourage business units to create services they use with the idea that they will be reused for company-wide benefit by other business units. In addition, though, those units creating services need to ensure that the services they create can meet the obligations to others who may reuse the service. This requires a layer of management, governance, and cooperation that might not exist prior to a commitment to SOA adoption. That said, the additional governance is far less costly in the larger scheme of efficiency afforded by an enterprise-wide SOA approach.

Open Source Software

In the software development community, it is widely held that there are two significant methodologies used by software providers to develop their products. While much of the software written throughout the history of computing has been packaged software that is developed with proprietary source code in a more closed development environment, the open source software movement has aimed to change this.

In its simplest definition, open source describes a particular type of software license designed to make a product's source code and other rights that would otherwise be retained by copyright holders available to the general public with little or no copyright restriction. By making the underlying software code used to create the product freely available as the software is designed, developed, and distributed, the original developer of the product is openly intending— like other open source developers—to share its production techniques and to encourage more collaborative approaches to tailoring other software products.

While the open source software cultural movement has roots back to the 1960s, it gained popularity and momentum in the late 1990s fueled by more widespread use and access to the Internet, which enabled more collaboration and sharing among independent developers in the software community. Open source software is often developed publicly and collaboratively. It has become widely adopted over the last decade and its advocates cite cost savings as a key benefit.

As a facilitator and advocate, The Open Source Initiative (OSI), a California public benefit corporation, was founded in 1998. The OSI oversees what it calls the Open Source Definition (OSD) and considers itself "the community-recognized body for reviewing licenses as OSD conformant." To that end, the OSI maintains the OSD, which is a set of guidelines to determine conformance with open source software.

The Open Source Definition according to The Open Source Initiative (also available at http://opensource.org/docs/osd) is composed of 10 criteria, and the distribution terms of open-source software must comply with these criteria:

1. *Free redistribution.* The license shall not restrict any party from selling or giving away the software as a component of an aggregate software distribution containing programs from several different sources. The license shall not require a royalty or other fee for such sale.
2. *Source code.* The program must include source code, and must allow distribution in source code as well as compiled form. Where some form of a product is not distributed with source code, there must be a well-publicized means of obtaining the source code for no more than a reasonable

reproduction cost preferably, downloading via the Internet without charge. The source code must be the preferred form in which a programmer would modify the program. Deliberately obfuscated source code is not allowed. Intermediate forms such as the output of a preprocessor or translator are not allowed.

3. *Derived works.* The license must allow modifications and derived works, and must allow them to be distributed under the same terms as the license of the original software.

4. *Integrity of the author's source code.* The license may restrict source code from being distributed in modified form only if the license allows the distribution of "patch files" with the source code for the purpose of modifying the program at build time. The license must explicitly permit distribution of software built from modified source code. The license may require derived works to carry a different name or version number from the original software.

5. *No discrimination against persons or groups.* The license must not discriminate against any person or group of persons.

6. *No discrimination against fields of endeavor.* The license must not restrict anyone from making use of the program in a specific field of endeavor. For example, it may not restrict the program from being used in a business, or from being used for genetic research.

7. *Distribution of license.* The rights attached to the program must apply to all to whom the program is redistributed without the need for execution of an additional license by those parties.

8. *License must not be specific to a product.* The rights attached to the program must not depend on the program's being part of a particular software distribution. If the program is extracted from that distribution and used or distributed within the terms of the program's license, all parties to whom the program is redistributed should have the same rights as those that are granted in conjunction with the original software distribution.

9. *License must not restrict other software.* The license must not place restrictions on other software that is distributed along with the licensed software. For example, the license

must not insist that all other programs distributed on the same medium must be open-source software.

10. *License must be technology-neutral.* No provision of the license may be predicated on any individual technology or style of interface.[7]

Open source methodologies have precedent in other industries. Early in the automotive industry, manufacturers created a licensing agreement whereby each company would develop their own technology and file patents, but would then share their patents without any financial consideration. This allowed legal access to new innovation that intended to help the industry as a whole.

Company IT groups that manage their company's many software applications and those who develop them are finding open source strategies to be increasingly attractive to the bottom line. In fact, some CIOs are committed to an entire technology infrastructure that's based on open source methodologies. For some smaller organizations, an open source development environment has provided them access to software and applications that they wouldn't have otherwise been able to afford and deploy. For other organizations, open source plays a part in at least some of their development environment. Figure 3.4 shows an overview of open source software development and distribution.

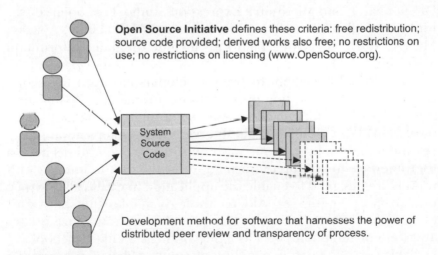

Open Source Initiative defines these criteria: free redistribution; source code provided; derived works also free; no restrictions on use; no restrictions on licensing (www.OpenSource.org).

System Source Code

Development method for software that harnesses the power of distributed peer review and transparency of process.

Figure 3.4   Open Source Software

Web Development and Mashups

Advances in web development tools coupled by the number of services that enable companies to create a basic web site have brought web development costs down significantly since the mid-1990s. Whereas early tools and methodologies required specialized developers to interpret and write code, today's commercially available tools allow WYSIWYG ("what you see is what you get") development, allowing less technically skilled knowledge workers in a company to update and modify web sites without the ongoing need for well-skilled web developers to handle the more routine updating. The technology community is fond of calling any of today's more contemporary development projects "Web 2.0" as a reference to the more contemporary tools and processes companies use to create web-enabled applications for internal and external customers (as opposed to the early web, which merely enabled relatively slow access to mostly text content).

All of this progress in web development has fueled, if not accelerated, the proliferation of not only web sites and the applications and information delivered on them, but the applications created within companies to optimize employee workflow and productivity. Simply put, the bulk of new corporate applications built today are created with Web 2.0 philosophies and tools. Examples of key web development tool providers include PC SOFT's WebDev, Adobe's Dreamweaver, and Microsoft's Expression Studio. Free open source tools are available as well, like the popular LAMP (Linux, Apache, MySQL, and PHP). Other platforms include the Java Platform and Microsoft's .NET.

A major advancement for web developers has been the evolution and use of application programming interfaces (APIs) in their software programming to allow other software to interact with their own. An API can "call" or request services from other software sources and web sites. In the same way that software applications need a user interface to interpret information for the user to interact with it, APIs are designed to enable the application to easily call information from other sources. API technology enables the sharing of information across web sites, like photos on photo-sharing sites and content and photos on social networking sites like Facebook.

APIs play a key part in enabling mashups, which allow users of a web site to see data presented from various sources and integrated to deliver value when they are all presented together. Much like the concept of a musical mashup, where pieces of completely different original works are woven together to create a completely new original work, software mashups leverage data from separate sources to create an altogether new application.

A basic example of a mashup targeting a consumer is how a real estate site might use APIs to call on various other applications to present real estate listings, while using other APIs to render map details related to a particular listing so that it appears next to the listing. Similarly, a weather web site might call on various sources of incoming weather data, and APIs would enable the web site to reference and present that data all in one place for the web site visitor. In these examples, the user of the web site may not necessarily know, or even need to know, that the data is being aggregated from various sources.

While many mashups are created for consumer markets, the concept has grown in popularity in enterprise environments. In the enterprise, a mashup allows richer application that can call on internal and external data with the intent to present information for better and more collaborative decision making. Given the stakes involved in a corporate setting, however, enterprise mashups require more sophistication. For example, they require more attention to security, access, and data governance. As a result, enterprise grade tools have emerged that facilitate mashups including IBM's QEDWiki, Yahoo's Pipes, Google's Mashup Editor, and Microsoft's Popfly.

Naturally, with so much interest in mashups, the market has expressed interest in developing standards. With that in mind, the Open Mashup Alliance (OMA) was formed in 2009 as "a consortium of individuals and organizations dedicated to the successful use of Enterprise Mashup technologies and adoption of an open language that promotes Enterprise Mashup intcroperability and portability."

The OMA defines enterprise mashups and their Enterprise Mashup Markup Language standard as follows:

> Enterprise Mashups combine and remix data from databases, spreadsheets, websites, Web Services, RSS/Atom feeds, and unstructured sources that deliver actionable information for better decision-making. The Open Mashup Alliance has been chartered to steward an open, free-to-use Enterprise Mashup Markup Language (EMML) that can reduce the risk and cost

of enterprise mashup implementations, improve mashup portability of mashup designs, and increase the interoperability of mashup solutions.[8]

Blending It All Together

The common thread that ties together all the complementary technologies reviewed in this chapter is the Internet. The Internet is enabling more widespread use of all of them and this increasing level of use in turn drives the speed and depth of development that we are seeing in these technologies. These technologies are literally evolving month by month. More and more of these technologies involve standards-based or open source platforms, that enable a wider body of users to contribute to their continued development.

Start-up companies and established companies are using various combinations of these technologies to create and deliver applications and services for internal use and for sale to external customers. Cloud computing providers use these technologies to deliver computing power to their customers at lower and lower cost points as they start to reap the rewards of larger and larger economies of scale. Both audiences–user companies as well as cloud computing providers–have been, and continue to be, key forces behind the continuous development of all of these technologies. Figure 3.5

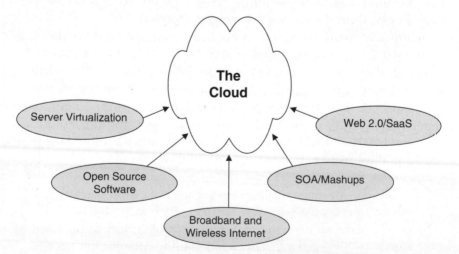

Figure 3.5   Cloud Computing Emerges from Combination of Technologies

illustrates this combination of *technologies that have given rise to cloud computing*.

Notes

1. Geoffrey A. Fowler and Ben Worthen, "The Internet Industry Is on a Cloud—Whatever That May Mean," *Wall Street Journal*, March 26, 2009.
2. International Data Corporation (IDC), September 2009.
3. Erica Naone "Conjuring Clouds," *MIT Technology Review*, July/August, 2009.
4. Stephen Cass "Briefing: Cloud Computing," *MIT Technology Review*, July/August, 2009.
5. Ellen Messmer, "Gartner: Server virtualization now at 18% of server workload," *Network World.com*, October 20, 2009.
6. Kenneth G. Brill, "Servers: Why Thrifty Isn't Nifty," Forbes.com, August 11, 2008.
7. The Open Source Initiative, www.opensource.org.
8. Ibid.

CHAPTER 4

Data Security and Service Reliability

Consider this quote by a cloud industry executive: "Any business leader worried about the security and reliability of their data in the cloud should remember that they've been trusting, saving, and storing their personal financial assets in an external, virtual banking cloud for years."

Will Your Cloud Service Provider Be Here Next Year?

This is a good question, and one that every executive should be asking. On one hand, there are highly reputable cloud service providers who are so well established—either from their previous lives, or because they are new but have grown to widespread use—that they are quite likely to be in this business for the foreseeable future. Amazon Web Services, IBM, HP, Salesforce.com, among many others, are strong players with solid futures.

On the other hand, for every one of the large players in cloud computing, there are hundreds of smaller players offering some type of cloud solution. Whether the provider you consider is large or small, every potential customer should exercise proper due diligence in the selection process that would include analysis of the company's financial stability, future prospects, and viability as a long-term and going concern.

Jeff Kaplan, Managing Director of THINKstrategies, a SaaS and cloud computing advisor, feels that key cloud providers are taking security and reliability quite seriously. In his white paper "The CIO's

Guide to Software as a Service,"[1] he says that unlike the traditional, on-premise software model that puts the burden of success on the customer, the SaaS subscription model places the burden on SaaS vendors to deliver reliable and secure services that meet the needs of their customers. According to Kaplan, the vendors' business depends on delivering quality services and safeguarding their customers' valuable data, so the leading SaaS vendors invest in state-of-the-industry service delivery and security technologies and certifications programs that include SAS 70 (the Statement on Auditing Standards 70), ISO standards, and Payment Card Identification (PCI). This requires the SaaS providers to implement extensive and well-documented security practices that govern their data center operations and personnel—including processes that regularly test facilities and staff.

All of this said, the most critical step in investigating the viability, reliability, and security of a cloud solution provider for the long term is the creation of a well-prepared request for proposal (RFP), which has several objectives. At the highest level, the RFP allows your organization to concisely compile all of the requirements of a particular technology initiative. Once those requirements are all agreed upon and determined, it then gives your organization an opportunity to formally request proposals from various bidders, and for the bidders to submit their proposals all using the same requirements.

A standard portion of any RFP is the request for information about the financial standing and viability of the vendor company. Gathering this information from bidding vendors is important with any RFP, but is particularly important with newer technologies where the players being considered are a mix of traditional vendors with long-standing brand recognition and reputation, and newer start-ups with smaller customer bases, less financial resources, credibility, and reputation.

Relevant information requested in the RFP can and should range from how long the company has been in business, the growth of the customer base and revenue, the company's available credit, and references from other customers. Ultimately, this information helps the potential customer assess and balance the value of the vendor's potential solution—which could appear to be significant—against the backdrop of the company's financial strength and future prospects, which could be shaky.

All of this might help a company make a decision like the following: Two vendors among a field of six are the strongest contenders based on the strength of their solution. One vendor is more diversified and has a longer-standing presence and track record of success. Its future viability, as demonstrated by information reported in the RFP as well as customer references, is relatively strong. The other vendor, with a more focused portfolio, less customers, and less experience in the field, has an even stronger potential solution, however, its prospects of weathering the ups and downs of challenges in the IT market, aren't nearly as great as the other vendor.

All of this makes selecting a vendor difficult. With new cloud computing vendors and solutions emerging (either from within larger, more established vendors, or as small, venture-funded start-ups), this makes the financial viability of all considered vendors particularly important.

What to Look for in a Good Service Provider

Once a vendor is selected to support a cloud computing initiative, a smart way for the organization to proceed is with a pilot project—a limited initiative that helps the organization move some computing to the cloud and minimizes risk because the project is smaller and manageable as a first-time effort. A pilot project also allows the organization to learn in the process. Simply put, if and when issues arise during a pilot, they will be much easier to resolve, and far less risky, if the footprint of the project is relatively small.

Preparing for a pilot project requires research and planning—and ultimately helps the organization understand the specifics to identify in a suitable provider. Naturally, this research will form the basis for preparing the RFP described earlier. As important as selecting a vendor, the analysis will force the organization to assess the ultimate business value of moving to the cloud in the first place.

Any move to the cloud should be based on a thorough situation/business analysis. The standard questions should be asked. Can a return be calculated on the investment? Can a longer-term return be anticipated? Does the technology perform as well as, if not better than, the existing internal platform? Is the cloud solution efficient, if not more efficient, than the existing environment?

In order to answer these questions, draw a circle around the users, applications, and business processes that will potentially use the cloud solution. From there, it shouldn't be difficult to analyze the costs of the existing solution compared to the cloud solution. Naturally, one should be careful to consider all costs and savings related to hardware, software, personnel, and any ancillary and on-going expenditures.

Then comes the harder part—assessing performance. While it's relatively easy to understand performance of the existing systems—their availability, redundancy, backup, recovery, latency, and the like—identifying the same for a cloud solution is a bit more difficult. The cloud services providers being considered need to allow a thorough audit of their application and systems performance. In a cloud solution, fundamentals like hardware and software environments, ISPs, and server locations can change over time, and so will the corresponding system response time and throughput. In order to determine if the cloud solution will perform at least as well as the existing solution, the cloud pro-vider will need to enable a cooperative performance audit. Ulti-mately, the audit will prove to be pivotal in determining if a particular vendor's solution is at least as efficient as the existing environment.

Elements of Good Data Security Policy

Security is arguably the top concern of companies when considering a move of data or computing resources to the cloud. Companies have grown accustomed to safeguarding data sitting in their own data centers, so getting used to the concept of proprietary data and applications sitting outside of traditional company jurisdictions presents worries, concerns, and challenges to not only data policies, but a company's well-entrenched culture and values.

With so many companies moving data and applications to the cloud, however, much thought is naturally being invested in ad-dressing these concerns. One organization in particular has addressed the matter in order to ensure that data in the cloud is widely safeguarded. The Cloud Security Alliance was formed in 2008 by a group of industry leaders in order to promote best practices in assuring security with cloud computing initiatives. The alliance intends to:

- Promote a common level of understanding between the consumers and providers of cloud computing regarding the necessary security requirements and attestation of assurance.
- Promote independent research into best practices for cloud computing security.
- Launch awareness campaigns and educational programs on the appropriate uses of cloud computing and cloud security solutions.
- Create consensus lists of issues and guidance for cloud security assurance.[2]

A major product of the Cloud Security Alliance's efforts is their publication of and updates to a document available on their web site entitled "Security Guidance for Critical Areas of Focus in Cloud."[3] The document provides users and vendors alike with a key source of specific recommendations in managing security policies and is a must read for technical teams investigating and implementing cloud solutions. The report's detailed guidance suggests the following:

- Determine exactly what data or function is being considered for the cloud.
- Assess how important the data or function is to the organization.
- Determine which of the following cloud options are acceptable: public; private (internal); private (external); community; hybrid.
- Evaluate the degree of control available to implement risk mitigations.
- Map out the flow of data in and out of the cloud to identify points of exposure to risk.[4]

In June 2008, analyst firm Gartner published a report called "Assessing the Security Risks of Cloud Computing" which identified seven security issues prospective buyers of cloud services should raise with potential vendors. An article in *Network World* entitled "Gartner: Seven Cloud-Computing Security Rrisks" recaps the advice:

1. *Privileged user access.* Sensitive data processed outside the enterprise brings with it an inherent level of risk, because

outsourced services bypass the "physical, logical, and personnel controls" IT shops exert over in-house programs. Get as much information as you can about the people who manage your data. "Ask providers to supply specific information on the hiring and oversight of privileged administrators, and the controls over their access," Gartner says.

2. *Regulatory compliance.* Customers are ultimately responsible for the security and integrity of their own data, even when it is held by a service provider. Traditional service providers are subjected to external audits and security certifications. Cloud computing providers who refuse to undergo this scrutiny are "signaling that customers can only use them for the most trivial functions," according to Gartner.

3. *Data location.* "When you use the cloud, you probably won't know exactly where your data is hosted. In fact, you might not even know what country it will be stored in. Ask providers if they will commit to storing and processing data in specific jurisdictions, and whether they will make a contractual commitment to obey local privacy requirements on behalf of their customers," Gartner advises.

4. *Data segregation.* Data in the cloud is typically in a shared environment alongside data from other customers. Encryption is effective but isn't a cure-all. "Find out what is done to segregate data at rest," Gartner advises. The cloud provider should provide evidence that encryption schemes were designed and tested by experienced specialists. "Encryption accidents can make data totally unusable, and even normal encryption can complicate availability," Gartner says.

5. *Recovery.* Even if you don't know where your data is, a cloud provider should tell you what will happen to your data and service in case of a disaster. "Any offering that does not replicate the data and application infrastructure across multiple sites is vulnerable to a total failure," Gartner says. Ask your provider if it has "the ability to do a complete restoration, and how long it will take."

6. *Investigative support.* Investigating inappropriate or illegal activity may be impossible in cloud computing, Gartner warns. "Cloud services are especially difficult to investigate, because logging and data for multiple customers may be co-located and may also be spread across an ever-changing set of hosts

and data centers. If you cannot get a contractual commitment to support specific forms of investigation, along with evidence that the vendor has already successfully supported such activities, then your only safe assumption is that investigation and discovery requests will be impossible."

7. *Long-term viability.* Ideally, your cloud computing provider will never go broke or get acquired and swallowed up by a larger company. But you must be sure your data will remain available even after such an event. "Ask potential providers how you would get your data back and if it would be in a format that you could import into a replacement application," Gartner says.[5]

Cyber Threats and Perimeter Security in Cloud Computing

". . . it is critical that cloud customers select the right cloud formations for their needs, to ensure they remain secure, able to collaborate safely with their selected parties as their evolving business needs require, and compliant to applicable regulatory requirements–including on the use and location of their data. The joy of the cloud model is that it can deliver great advantages, but only if you know where in the different formations of cloud you need to be in order to achieve the right flexibility for your business needs . . ."[6]

—*The Jericho Forum's Cloud Cube Model*

Prior to cloud computing, companies created perimeter security by installing hardened firewalls to block unwanted traffic trying to access the corporate network. They also established restricted access through passwords and education to block malicious access to their traditional data centers. With far fewer mobile users and with virtually all data resident in-house, this strategy made sense. But times have changed. Since today's cloud computing model moves company-owned data outside the traditional corporate security boundaries, and since professional hackers have proven that they will continue to explore and exploit weaknesses, companies need to take a fresh look at their security strategy, objectives, and defenses.

While perimeter security has been a foundation of corporate information security planning and implementation, some corporate security officers have advocated the need for a more contemporary philosophy that embraces the changes resulting from widespread Internet access and the resulting corporate security vulnerabilities. As early as 2001, some security experts began discussing the need for what they call "deperimeterization." Today, a group called the Jericho Forum has advanced that philosophy for cloud computing models. They have put forth a deperimeterized approach to security. As shown in Figure 4.1, this approach, called the Cloud Cube Model, identifies and defines four criteria to differentiate cloud formations from one another.

The four criteria include:

1. *Internal versus external.* If it is within your own physical boundary, then it is internal; if it is not within your own physical boundary, then it is external.
2. *Open versus proprietary.* Proprietary means that the organization providing the service is keeping the means of provision

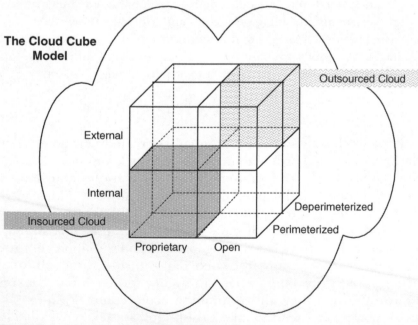

Figure 4.1   The Cloud Cube Model

under their ownership. As a result, when operating in clouds that are proprietary, the Jericho Forum suggests you may not be able to move to another cloud supplier without significant effort or investment. Often the more innovative technology advances occur in the proprietary domain. As such the proprietor may choose to enforce restrictions through patents and by keeping the technology involved a trade secret. Clouds that are open are using technology that is not proprietary, meaning that there are likely to be more suppliers, and the Jericho Forum suggests you are not as constrained in being able to share your data and collaborate with selected parties using the same open technology. Open services tend to be those that are widespread and consumerized, and most likely a published open standard, for example, email (SMTP).

3. *Outsourced versus insourced.* Outsourced means the service is provided by a third party; insourced means the service is provided by your own staff under your control.

4. *Perimeterized versus deperimeterized.* Perimeterized implies continuing to operate within the traditional IT perimeter, often signaled by "network firewalls." As has been discussed in previous published Jericho Forum papers, this approach inhibits collaboration. In effect, when operating in the perimeterized areas, the Jericho Forum suggests you may simply extend your own organization's perimeter into the external cloud computing domain using a VPN and operating the virtual server in your own IP domain, making use of your own directory services to control access. Then, when the computing task is completed you can withdraw your perimeter back to its original traditional position. The Jericho Forum considers this type of system perimeter to be a traditional, though virtual, perimeter. Deperimeterized, assumes that the system perimeter is architected following the principles outlined in the Jericho Forum's Commandments and Collaboration Oriented Architectures (COA) Framework. The terms *microperimeterization* and *macro-perimeterization* will likely be in active use here—for example, in a deperimeterized frame the data would be encapsulated with metadata and mechanisms that would protect the data from inappropriate usage. COA-enabled systems allow secure collaboration. In a deperimeterized environment an organization can collaborate securely

with selected parties (business partner, customer, supplier, and outworker) globally over any COA capable network.[7]

Encryption: The Next Frontier of Data Security

Many organizations have been reluctant to move to cloud computing due to regulatory restrictions that prohibit them from using the cloud for storing sensitive data, or due to concerns about the privacy and security of data in the cloud. A recent article in *CIO* magazine put it like this, "There's no doubt that cloud computing is dominating today's IT conversation among C-level security executives. Whether they're lured by its compelling cost savings or its perceived advantages, security leaders are probing the capabilities and restrictions of the cloud. At the same time, security and compliance concerns remain issues holding large enterprises back from capitalizing on the cloud's benefits."[8]

To address these concerns a new class of data security products is appearing. These new data security products employ data encryption to keep the data secure. Even if unauthorized parties get through the other security measures and get access to the data, it will be to no avail if they can't read that data. Even if data is copied or stolen, if it is well encrypted, it will be useless unless those stealing the data can also secure a copy of the encryption key that will unlock the data and enable them to read it. There is a new class of encryption-based data security products that puts the enterprise administrator in control of powerful measures to protect an organization's data.

These products specifically address the limitations and concerns of using SaaS and other cloud applications to handle sensitive corporate data. Implemented as an appliance on the enterprise LAN/ WAN or as a cloud service, these encryption products encrypt data used by SaaS application before it is transmitted from the enterprise to the SaaS provider. Authorized people using these SaaS applications are not affected by the encryption and remain largely unaware of this process. Their data is encrypted as it leaves their internal company systems and, when stored on the SaaS provider's servers, it is unreadable by anyone without the encryption key. Database theft and regulatory compliance issues are then addressed as all sensitive data remains undecipherable when in transmission and at rest outside the enterprise firewall.

Developers of cloud applications don't need to implement any special code in their applications to provide them with this level of security and regulatory compliance. This encryption software can be added to an application as a service (SOA or SaaS) and it will encrypt and secure data as it flows through the application. Some people have coined the acronym VPS or "virtual private SaaS" to describe this new category of encryption-based data security software.[9]

Contracts, Service-Level Agreements, and Guarantees

As with any newly contracted service—whether it's for information technology or not—organizations committed to moving to a cloud-based solution should have a knowledgeable lawyer review their cloud service provider contract both during the negotiations and before final signature. There are many law firms that specialize in legal considerations related to information technology implementations, and some are familiar with the nuances and new ground encountered by deployments in the cloud.

Service-level agreements (SLAs) have become more widely used in many industries over the last few decades and, of course, they can and should be used well in managing service-level expectations and requirements from cloud service providers. Simply put, SLAs are comprised of the language—in the context of an overall master services agreement—that clearly specifies for the customer and the service provider what's expected of the provider and customer. These details are valuable to both parties because they provide a legally binding reference document to help manage the ongoing service level, including specific metrics and measures of performance along with pricing tables. Like any legally binding agreement, the objective is to protect both parties and to prevent challenges and disputes in managing service levels. A well-written SLA will actually prevent problems before they can significantly impact ongoing business operations.

Customers should be aware that providers will have engaged legal advice in constructing their proposed master agreement and SLA. With their own best interests in mind, customers should also involve a corporate legal representative to review the document and provide advice prior to signature. In this process, it is important for the agreement to be written plainly and clearly, and for the customer parties who will be managing the business enabled by the services to have provided input, especially in the form of asking "what if" questions that may impact business performance.

SLAs can be constructed in several ways, and there is much guidance available on the best way to approach them, but generally, there is consensus that an SLA document should cover at least the following basic sections:

- *Overview.* This section should briefly identify the parties entering the agreement and concisely describe the general nature of the agreed-upon services purchased.
- *Scope of work.* A more elaborate overview, this section is also commonly called the SOW and forms an important part of the agreement that clearly details the services provided to the customer.
- *Performance measures.* Good preparation and input from both parties is required to create this critical portion of the agreement. Measures appearing in this section should fairly and reasonably identify metrics that will be continuously monitored throughout the term of the agreement including items as varied as uptime, throughput, and the number of end-user customers that can be served simultaneously. While the provider will have ideas on what's best to measure, the business buying the service should incorporate and negotiate to include critical measurements that help it meet its business objectives—and that serve customers reliably and securely. These items can and should be very specific to the business enabled by the cloud provider. In cases where the service is extremely critical to second-to-second business success, it may be worth investing in a third-party service that can help monitor and report on service levels.
- *Managing problem resolution.* This section should detail the agreed-upon process whereby the customer can alert the provider to problems along with the timeliness of response and the procedures for how the problem will be resolved. By putting this process in writing, both parties are then clear on what will take place when a problem arises. The provider will likely want protections here as well that ensure they can address any problems that might be inadvertently caused by the customer.

- *Fee structure.* This section should very clearly and simply state the fees being charged by the provider to the customer along with payment terms.
- *Customer obligations.* So that the provider is given the best opportunity to meet all of their obligations of the agreement, the provider will require that the customer remain obligated to providing needed information on a timely basis. This area of the agreement will be highly specialized and should detail the specific information and related processes to exchange information between the customer and the provider.
- *Warranties.* This is the area of the agreement where the customer wants the provider to make guarantees and to specify how they will make good on those guarantees if, for any reason, the provider can't meet the obligations of the service they guarantee. Essentially, it's where the provider is held accountable for nonperformance during the agreement and where the customer can seek relief for that non-performance. Naturally, this can be a highly negotiated point before the agreement is finalized where the provider wants to minimize the guarantees and, conversely, the customer wants some ironclad remedies where they may have specific concerns if or when the provider doesn't fulfill service obligations. This is also an area where the customer can ask the provider to warrant simple but important facts. An example would be warranting that the provider has the legal ability to provide the needed business services in all of the applicable geographic locations.
- *Security.* Since security is of major concern to customers when implementing cloud solutions, it's a good idea for the SLA to clearly describe the security capabilities of the solution along with the procedures that will take place in the event of a security breach.
- *Compliance.* Some customers are governed by industry-specific regulatory requirements restricting how information is shared and any processes to deal with these issues, and they should be detailed in this section to ensure that the provider will be conforming—and how it will be dealt with if a problem arises.
- *Confidential information and intellectual property.* This section provides the opportunity for both parties to clearly define the respective intellectual property they own that is not the right

of the other party. Importantly, it is also where they require the other party to treat specified information that may be exchanged as confidential. If information is to enter the hands of third parties on behalf of the provider, the customer will want the provider to secure confidentiality guarantees from the third party.

- *Liability protection.* Since the cloud involves customer data that can sit in multiple locations and be processed by multiple companies, the technology industry finds itself on new legal ground with liability protections. Of significant concern to the customer are the implications of a breach to a cloud provider's security, and what court-ordered restrictions might potentially be placed on processing that data in the event of an unforeseen legal challenge. With that in mind, the agreement should specify all of the locations where customer data might potentially reside—and provide guarantees that all of those handlers of the data (which may include other providers) are in compliance with regulatory requirements. Customers should require language that helps avoid any legal interruption to ongoing business operations or access to their own data should a breach or legal challenge materialize. Given the changing cloud landscape and emerging precedents, it's critically important for customers to engage relevant legal advice at the earliest stages of the RFP process to ensure the most contemporary protections are applied to the agreement—and that providers are aware of the customer's legal requirements.

- *Regular review.* To make sure that unforeseen issues have an opportunity to be aired throughout the contract period, a scheduled set of review meetings provides an opportunity to not only maintain a good working relationship, but to adjust the agreement as necessary should changes in business circumstances warrant.

- *Termination.* As is standard in legally binding agreements, the SLA should provide language describing how the agreement can be terminated by either party, and the procedures to follow, including how data is transitioned to a new environment along with the related schedule.

- *Implementation.* This portion of the agreement describes the schedule the parties have agreed upon to start the transition to the new service, the date intended to launch the service to end-user customers, and key milestones and deliverables required in either direction along the way.

Negotiating Service and Pricing

Many cloud computing observers argue that cost is often the primary driver for considering cloud initiatives. They are correct that the cloud can offer some cost-effective alternatives to, say, owning and operating 100 servers to achieve a particular business objective. They also point out that the amount of time and energy consumed by worrying about hardware, maintenance, uptime, and reliance on internal data center resources can represent a sizable opportunity cost for the business. That said, there is every reason to take a very close look at cloud computing's delivery and pricing models despite what may initially appear to be a good value. All of this starts with a careful negotiation that can prove to be a strategic factor in not only developing a good working relationship with a cloud provider, but in establishing fair pricing models for both parties.

While contracts can be laden with seemingly clinical language and endless legal terms, written agreements should be based on the outcome of very practical business discussions between the two parties. The best place to start is making sure that the potential provider understands that the customer is looking for a partnership, rather than what can often become a standoffish procurement/supplier relationship. This approach can be critical to an ongoing, fair, and friendly working relationship.

Once a fair and friendly tone of negotiations is established, it becomes much easier for cloud service customers to state their expectations of the negotiation process and what they feel the steps in the process should be. In their most basic form, they can include:

- Identifying requirements in plain business language.
- Folding those requirements into a more formal requirements document.
- Reserving time for the customer to seek some third-party expertise.

For the provider, knowing these steps up front becomes valuable as it minimizes the amount of guesswork and related time the cloud service provider might waste in trying to understand the customer's preferred negotiation process. It also gives the provider an opportunity to weigh in on that process and add value based on their own experience. The key here is to avoid dwelling on specific wording of contract language (which will come later) and to keep the conversations friendly, practical, and based on business goals.

Once negotiation expectations are established, it's time to develop the relatively short list of customer requirements. Frank discussion with the potential provider should occur, focusing on items essential for business success. This is the critical time to sort them out—and to understand if there are nuances from the provider regarding what can and cannot be delivered. It is also the juncture where the customer has to critically assess if some requirements are unrealistic. The customer has to decide on whether—by accommodating the provider's particular capabilities on a specific negotiating point—it will (or will not) seriously impact the customer's ongoing business. Again, the key here is for the customer to be pragmatic about what must eventually appear in the contract versus what they would like to see in the contract. This means compromising on some hoped-for service requirements that are not actually critical requirements. A consistent look at "what really matters," and what other, possibly noncritical business factors are actually motivating a particular requirement, is important here.

Once the general business requirements are established and fundamentally agreed upon by the customer and the provider, the provider will want to drop the requirements into their standard agreement framework. The customer should then audit the requirements in that legal context to make sure that the intent and meaning aren't altered by legal terminology.

A critical step takes place next: getting outside perspective. A lawyer familiar with these types of agreements should review it to make sure that critical points are not missed. Just as important, however, is for the customer to get some peer review (depending upon desired confidentiality) of the business requirements, the pricing, or the entire agreement, from some trusted colleagues who have purchased similar services. This process can reveal not only pitfalls to avoid, but insight on pricing models successfully negotiated by other companies.

Performance Penalties and Restitution Clauses

The sheer volume and popularity of different contractual arrangements whereby companies buy technology services (as opposed to buying just software and hardware that they then operate on their own) has created an environment full of providers adept at negotiating, if not limiting, penalties they might incur for missed performance. On the other hand, all of this provides valuable lessons in how to apply simple penalties and incentives that deliver the best value. The following are some critical tips customers should consider as they navigate this part of their contract negotiation with a cloud provider:

- *Simplicity is better for all.* In this classic application of "less is more," customers should focus on incorporating only a few pragmatic penalties and incentives and describe them clearly and succinctly. In addition, by defining performance penalties in business terms and relating service levels directly to business processes (rather than to the related technology performance), the customer is able to hold the provider accountable on what really matters to business success. While there may be temptation to focus on uptime and throughput because these are easy performance levels to measure, it is also important to keep the cloud service provider clearly aware of what performance levels or potential problems can truly have a negative impact on the customer's ongoing business operations and become serious threats to joint success.
- *Review potential penalties before signature.* It's one thing to establish the penalties in the contract, but by reviewing the established penalties face-to-face with the provider prior to contract signature, the provider is given a clear understanding that the customer takes performance seriously. In addition, it makes sense to discuss performance and penalties in a regular review cycle that can be specified in the contract.
- *Use care in balancing incentives and penalties.* No one understands the customer's business better than the customer. With that in mind, the customer should not assume that well-meaning but poorly defined incentives and penalties can prevent a well-intentioned contract from running into trouble over time. For example, after a contract is signed, it

can be very easy for the customer to ignore contract details and focus on their business, and for the provider to focus on simply providing service (and spending time on other customers). During this time, seemingly minor, but regular, performance shortfalls and penalties can begin to occur. All of this can be easy to ignore, but it's a sign of a problem that needs to be fixed.

- *Focus on preventing problems.* Well-designed penalties should focus on identifying and alerting all parties so as to react quickly and avoid problems before they become serious. If a problem occurs, it should be a signal for the provider to solve the problem for the longer term, rather than allowing it to continue by incurring a soft but ongoing penalty. One way to accomplish this is to accelerate penalties for problems that persist over time or that the provider is lax in addressing. While this may seem harsh, it causes the provider to clearly understand that the agreement has no tolerance for unresolved problems.

- *Understand that you get what you pay for.* The customer should adopt a stance of being a business realist and avoid temptations to hold the provider to unrealistic service levels that aren't truly required to maintain business operations. And the customer should be willing to pay a fair price for the service levels sought. Demands for flawed and excessive requirements with stiff penalties will not only reduce the field of willing providers, but can result in the customer's overpaying for a service that could be had at a lower cost if requirements were simply more realistic.

Notes

1. Jeff Kaplan, "The CIO's Guide to Software as a Service: A Primer for Understanding and Maximizing the Value of SaaS Solutions," white paper from THINKstrategies http://thinkstrategies.com/researchpublications/whitepapers.html.
2. Cloud Security Alliance, www.cloudsecurityalliance.org/About.html.
3. Cloud Security Alliance, "Security Guidance for Critical Areas of Focus in Cloud Computing V2.1," December 2009, www.cloudsecurityalliance.org/csaguide.pdf.
4. Ibid.
5. Jon Brodkin, "Gartner: Seven Cloud-Computing Security Risks," *Network World,* July 2, 2008.

6. "Cloud Cube Model: Selecting Cloud Formations for Secure Collaboration, Version 1.0," April 2009, www.opengroup.org/jericho/cloud_cube_model_v1.0.pdf.
7. Ibid.
8. Jim Hietala, "Compliance under a Cloud," CIO.com February 24, 2010.
9. This concept was recently recognized as one of 10 finalists for the RSA Innovation Sandbox contest at the RSA Conference 2010 (https://365.rsaconference.com/docs/DOC-2392). Navajo Systems at www.NavajoSystems.com is one of the companies now offering VPS security software.

CHAPTER

Moving to the Cloud: When and Where

Internet-based technology is driving economic change at a level not seen since the spread of industrial technology in the late nineteenth and early twentieth centuries. What became known as "Web 2.0" and the business and consumer applications it spawned have continued to evolve. What has emerged is now known as cloud computing, software-as-a-service (SaaS), and social media. Since there's but a short history of using these technologies, they continue to converge and morph. We have much yet to learn, but it is quite clear that they are leading to disruptive changes in the way we communicate with each other and in the IT infrastructures that companies use to support their business operations.

The spread of cloud computing is an excellent example of the phenomenon known as "creative destruction," which was popularized by the economist Joseph Schumpeter.[1] Schumpeter pointed out that in capitalist economies, there are waves of change where the introduction of a new technology or new process for doing things upsets and replaces the previously dominant technology along with the people and companies who used that technology. Cloud computing is having this effect on vendors who sell traditional versions of computing technology and on the people who make their living operating traditional computing technology.

Companies that have large investments in traditional in-house computing technology will not abandon those investments immediately, nor should they. The transition of companies to cloud-based technology will be quicker for some and slower for others depending on their individual circumstances. But the change will happen. History shows over and over again that resistance to the spread of new technologies is almost always futile, and often fatal. People and companies that resist are finally forced out of business and replaced by others that do adopt new technology. Clearly the best strategy for people and companies is to actively explore the opportunities for cloud computing and begin appropriate projects to gain experience in its use and to understand its strengths and weaknesses.

A Business Strategy Based on Agility

On one hand, cloud computing can be considered primarily as a cost-saving technology that's used here and there on cost-cutting projects and for quick fixes to provide point solutions to specific operational problems. On the other hand, cloud computing can be understood in the context of an overall business strategy based on agility and responsiveness. Cloud computing certainly provides cost savings in some situations, but cost savings is not the most important benefit. The real value of cloud computing is the way in which it can be used to support an overall strategy designed to create agility for the business.

Companies that create a foundational business strategy based on agility put responsiveness before efficiency. This strategy emphasizes the ability to make continuous incremental changes and adjustments in operating procedures so the company can respond as new business conditions unfolds. It also emphasizes continuous exploration of new business opportunities along with rapid growth into new markets when it is sensed that they will be profitable.

An Example of Business Agility

Here is a case in point. Suppose a company, GrowMore Corporation, spots an opportunity to leverage its existing expertise and supplier relationships to launch a new product line for a market adjacent to its traditional spaces. In order to do this, the company wants to set up a new business unit with branch offices in key geographical locations. It wants to locate sales offices in these areas and wants to support the sales staff with a customer relationship management (CRM) system that enables them to prospect for customers, create presentations and proposals, and follow up with prospective customers in a timely and organized manner. Grow-More Corporation also wants to collect sales and prospecting information from all the regional offices and store it in a single database at headquarters to enable overall reporting and tracking of sales and business development activities.

The new product line will need some customization for individual customers so that it best fits unique needs, but GrowMore Corporation does not want to staff all these offices with engineers for this. Instead of sending engineers out with salespeople to make calls on prospect companies, the company wants to establish video-conferencing capabilities. This way, the salesperson on site with the customer or prospect can easily interview the customer—with the engineer participating by videoconference—in order to collect the information needed to configure the product.

In the old days, this would have been more complicated. Managers of the new start-up business unit would have submitted a support request to the company IT group. The IT group would then send out a business analyst to evaluate the request and study the needs of the new business unit. Then, the request would be prioritized against requests from other business units and, since existing business units typically get priority in the allocation of available IT resources, the start-up unit would likely have to wait until the next budget cycle before it could get funding for the IT services it needs.

When the funding and IT resources eventually became available, there would be a process of designing and developing the needed software or evaluating possible packaged software solutions. This would be followed by purchasing and installing the needed hardware and communications networks—and finally the rollout of the new system and accompanying user training. During that time, months or even years would have passed. In many cases the window of opportunity for the new business would have closed and the solution delivered would be too late or it would not effectively address business needs that had evolved and changed during the time it took to build and deploy the system.

Alternatively, management of the new start-up business unit today can go directly to relevant cloud service providers and start using one of their SaaS offerings within a matter of a few hours—or a few days at most. And unlike the old days, there isn't any big up-front cost involved—and no capital expense allocation needed—resulting in the cost of operating the systems varying according to amount of usage. If the business idea doesn't work out, there is no sunk capital cost and just a bit of expended system operating costs. If the new business does succeed, then operating costs are easily funded by sales revenue.

In this case, cloud solutions enabled a straightforward way to use videoconferencing and an SaaS application to quickly deploy a solution and respond to market need. Moreover, it can be adjusted on the fly as needs change.

Implications of Cloud-Enabled Business Agility

This lowers the cost of sales for that new business unit in a way that then makes it possible and profitable to go after smaller deals that weren't profitable before. The company can then build a base of business from many smaller deals that might be easier to land, instead of going after just the larger projects, and fighting all the competition going after that business. These are the benefits of using an agile business strategy and the technology that enables it. The case study at the end of this chapter further illustrates this principle.

Cloud computing has great cost-cutting potential in certain situations, but it's important to keep the larger business strategy in mind. The agility benefits far outweigh the purely cost-saving benefits. If a company's strategy calls for it to improve its ability to bring new products to market and improve its capability to expand geographically and open new offices, then cloud computing is a powerful technology to help meet those objectives.

Using cloud technology to enable new business formation and new product development creates newly found speed and opportunity for multinational small and medium businesses (SMBs). Today, powered by cloud technologies, SMBs can now be truly global when 10 years ago they couldn't afford the integrated IT infrastructure to support global operations. For instance, SMBs can now open a new sales office in countries around the world and then quickly conduct local sales campaigns in a way that was unthinkable before. Today, opening new country sales offices simply means adding local people to use a cloud-based CRM package and a cloud-based teleconferencing system. Specialists at company headquarters can then back up sales people with in-depth technical support without having to fly people around the world to meet with clients.

Using the Cloud for Business Advantage

Bernard Golden, CEO of HyperStratus, is a practitioner and speaker who specializes in cloud computing and related technologies. He also writes a popular blog entitled "Virtualization and Cloud Advisor" for *CIO* magazine.[2] He draws an insightful analogy between the early adoption of the Internet by business and the growing business use of cloud computing:

> At a certain point in time, the technology vendor community, especially startups, just caught fire about the Internet. They were convinced that, once experienced, no one could avoid adopting their work lives to the Internet. At that same point in time, mainstream IT looked at the Internet with a skeptical eye, focusing on its shortcomings. At that time, I heard statements like "nobody is going to let their data cross insecure public networks" and "Nobody is going to put real business function-ality out on the Web." Of course, the indisputable benefits of the Internet overwhelmed the dubious responses. As we look back now, the chaos and cynicism is hard to remember, but believe me, it was there—and strong. But those attitudes didn't stand a chance against easy access to information, and I think it's unlikely that a jaundiced view of cloud computing is going to prevail, either.[3]

Companies need IT infrastructures that enable them to operate more efficiently and that will also accommodate continuous, incre-mental changes in business operations. To that end, many compa-nies are already using server virtualization and some are also using service-oriented architecture (SOA) to better leverage their existing IT investments and get additional flexibility and responsiveness from their existing systems infrastructure.

Companies are now at the point where they need to move beyond an internal focus directed at maximizing use of IT resources to an external focus on supporting collaboration and new product development through use of cloud computing. Companies are moving from internally focused SOA projects to externally focused web-oriented architecture (WOA) projects where they begin using SaaS applications and combine them with internal applications that support collaboration with other companies to drive mutual growth.

This will happen because cloud and SaaS vendors are becoming more and more like utilities, offering reliable computing power and basic applications like email, enterprise resource planning (ERP), CRM, and a growing array of industry-specific applications. Over the coming years, these vendors will develop economies of scale and expertise that enables them to offer their services at a much lower cost than what most companies would spend to deliver those services internally.

Because of this, and over the coming years, companies will outsource more and more of their basic IT operations in order to better manage their costs for basic IT services. This will in turn enable companies to shift more of their time and attention to leveraging IT to add value to their products and provide meaningful differentiation in the eyes of their customers. IT will be used to deliver much more concentrated competitive advantage than ever before.

Cloud computing thrives in entrepreneurial environments where leapfrogging the competition is a daily motivator. Innovators need tools that fit their fast pace, their work-anywhere mentality, and their collaborative instincts. Cloud computing sets the stage for corporate innovation. Freed from lengthy implementation projects, moribund legacy applications, and armies of consultants, IT personnel can turn cloud computing into a competitive advantage.

Cloud computing offers significant advantages in its low startup costs and quick delivery of computing resources, as well as its pay-as-you-go cost structure. In addition, it offers ease of management, scalability of systems as needs grow, and device and location independence so people can access these systems from many different devices from a PC to a virtualized desktop to an iPad to a smart phone like a Blackberry or iPhone. And finally, cloud computing enables rapid innovation in companies to respond to evolving markets.

Many SaaS vendors and cloud service providers come to enterprise IT from consumer-facing IT environments, which means they are already focused on providing a customer-friendly interface to make their software and services easy to learn and use. They're also continuously integrating with mobile devices like Blackberries, iPhones, netbooks, electronic book readers and iPads—all of which are quickly becoming the new interface between people and the online world.

Business Applications with the Greatest Potential

To determine which applications could work well in the cloud, a good place to start is by applying a pain versus gain measurement. If your company is a start-up operation, then almost by definition most applications will be good candidates for cloud computing because of the advantages described in the example of GrowMore Corporation earlier in this chapter, and because the pain will be relatively minimal.

If your company is an established business with an existing infrastructure of in-house systems, then good candidates for potential cloud computing are environments involving:

- Stand-alone applications with a low business risk if something happens and the system goes down, or if the system data were compromised or stolen.
- Applications that are expected to have highly volatile and hard-to-predict workloads.
- Situations requiring collaboration and information sharing with an extended value chain of business partners.
- Applications where there is a need to perform periodic data analysis on high volumes of data.
- A platform to try out scenarios quickly and at low cost, to field test a new application system, or to create test and development environments for building new systems.
- Situations where there is a need to conserve capital expenditures.

Specific examples of stand-alone and low-risk applications are: a simple wiki blog site to support information sharing and knowledge management within a company; a system to allow people in field offices to collect and share data and update business planning models; and a system for use by the human resources group to pilot the use of a new recruiting process.

A specific example of an application with high volatility and usage patterns that are hard to predict is when a company launches a new product or a new product promotion and creates a web site to support that effort. If the site will be up for only six months or so and will be prone to high spikes in traffic volume, then the organization should question why they would want to spend the money and resources to sustain the site indefinitely—and why it should tie up internal systems infrastructure to support the peaks in usage volumes when that infrastructure will be underutilized during the nonpeak times.

A fast food restaurant chain might decide to promote special low-priced value meals by establishing a web site where customers can check for specials and search for the location of restaurants offering them. The site would be heavily accessed when certain specials are promoted, but it can be hard for the chain to predict the usage volume in advance, hence the attractiveness of running this application in the cloud. In this case, the company could employ a cloud service provider to set up the web site, which would be brought live quickly. The cloud service provider could provision the site with computing power and data storage capacity as needed and on demand. This way the company would pay only for the actual usage it incurred, its usage costs would drop during periods of lower customer activity, and the company would be guaranteed system capacity and availability during peak promotional periods.

Clouds also make sense where business is conducted based on shared data and where rapid feedback is needed. An example is a health care company that wants to share data on patient care and outcomes with a network of pharmaceutical companies and medical service providers. The health care company can make the data anonymous, blanking out the names of patients and then loading the data into a cloud-based system where all relevant parties can access the data and apply cloud-based analytics to sift through the data for important patterns and trends.

Applications where there is a need to perform periodic data analysis on high volumes of data are also good candidates for cloud computing. An energy company conducting geographical analysis to search for new oil fields could set up the compute intensive portions of this operation using a cloud-based system. When large databases of information come in from its field exploration units, the company could then ship this data up to the cloud, where it would be processed and the results returned for in-house analysis. The company could strip out location-related data so even if the data were stolen, it would not reveal sensitive information about where a promising new oil field might be located. And the company would pay only for the computing resources used for the job when the job was run–and avoid tying up money in idle infrastructure when there are no jobs to run.

Many companies are already using cloud solutions (infra-structure-as-a-service [IaaS] and platform-as-a-service [PaaS]) to quickly provide their in-house application development groups with testing and development environments. Instead of going through all the expense and time of purchasing the hardware and software needed to develop new systems, the development groups of these companies can get what they need immediately and only pay for it as long as their need lasts. As one senior enterprise architect at a major corporation put it, "You can buy a gift card on Amazon and use it to set up your own data center."[4] Cloud service providers like Amazon, Google, Hewlett-Packard, IBM, Microsoft, Rackspace, and others offer immediate provisioning like this.

Risk Considerations with the Cloud

As discussed in Chapter 4, there are a number of issues to consider when deciding on which applications to push to the cloud—and which cloud service providers to hire. Those issues and their related risks tend to fall into three basic categories: system and data security; performance management and service-level agreements; and vendor lock-in.

System and data security is the most frequently discussed risk since many worry that data placed in the cloud could be compromised or stolen by third parties. Yet it's important to view the risks in context of the current state of security that already exists in many companies. Most companies face data security issues that, while significant, are defended by systems less hardened than elaborate defenses of cloud service providers. Moreover, in-house data center operations are perceived as cost centers and, as a result, are always under pressure to cut costs, which ultimately means that not all of their security issues are adequately funded or supported.

With cloud service providers and SaaS vendors, data center operations and security are mission-critical to customer retention and profits, so these companies are far more inclined to invest in more than adequate security. And because their systems live in the cloud outside of corporate firewalls, they are attacked just as much, if not more, than most corporate infrastructures providing them with more experience than that of the average corporation.

Ultimately, the greatest security threat to systems and data, whether behind a corporate firewall or in the cloud, is what's called "social engineering"—the various and illicit practices used to interact with system users, data center operators, and help desk staff to illegally gain access to passwords and user IDs. There are many, continuously evolving methods used to trick employees and customers into giving away passwords and IDs to unauthorized parties, who then use this information to gain access to corporate data. Anyone considering a cloud deployment should remember that corporate IT groups are just as vulnerable to social engineering as cloud service providers and that protecting against social engineering is more a matter of managing human nature and behavior and maintaining effective policies for administering system access information.

Performance management of cloud-based systems is a subject that can make in-house IT staff uneasy. They are used to having more direct control over the actual computer and communications hardware and operating systems that drive the systems their companies have traditionally used. As a result, many are concerned that once systems are moved to a cloud environment, there will be no way to monitor and control the user response times and other performance characteristics. There is a sentiment that companies will just have to accept whatever performance levels the cloud service vendor may offer and make the best of it. That said, since high levels of performance and satisfied customers are central to the profitability of cloud service providers, they are inherently investing in technology that allows customers to monitor and manage many of the operating parameters of cloud-based systems. Cloud service providers are working with technology companies (like Akamai, Cisco Systems, F5, IBM, and Nimsoft among others) to design and install technology that monitors and displays real time information showing how well a given cloud application is performing. This technology enables the in-house IT staff to respond and make adjustments as system slowdowns and other problems materialize.

Performance management technology will continue to improve as cloud usage becomes more widespread. Technical problems have technical answers, and technical advances can happen quickly when there is sufficient demand. Performance management is rightly a concern of cloud customers—but it's not an obstacle that should prevent companies from making effective use of cloud systems and services.

Service-level agreements (SLAs) that guarantee specific levels of systems performance are constantly evolving. At present, cloud service providers and SaaS vendors do not offer strict guarantees on their service levels and when service outages do occur, they offer to reimburse customers for the cost of their services during the period of the outage. They are not inclined to pay penalties that would reimburse customers for loss of business revenue or costs they incur because of a service outage.

Context is important and it's important to remember that, in many cases, there is no formal measurement of the service levels provided by in-house IT groups. In-house systems go down or their response time slows down and people in a company just accept that as a fact of life.

The quality of in-house systems performance is directly related to the sophistication and training of in-house IT organizations. Certainly large corporations can afford large and well-trained IT staff and sophisticated data centers, but many (maybe even most) companies get by with underfunded data centers, poor automation, and understaffed IT operations. IT staff at these companies do the best they can with what they have, but they also make no guarantees about the quality of their service or the reliability of uptime for their systems. For these companies, a cloud provider could very well create an improvement in the quality of service.

Before stepping into the cloud, companies need to assess their risks associated with vendor lock-in. Cloud computing can often use a systems architecture different than the one used by the traditional in-house systems, so once a system is moved to the cloud, it isn't always a simple matter to bring it back in-house or to move it to another cloud. Before selecting a cloud provider or a SaaS vendor, it is critical to evaluate the stability and longevity of that company. It is just important to understand their pricing model and understand the likely ongoing costs associated with using their applications to run your business.

And once again, context is important. Lock-in already exists with traditional in-house systems and software. Once a company makes a commitment to use an ERP system and installs the software, there is a large degree of lock-in that comes along with that decision. It is expensive and time consuming to install an ERP system, and once it is done it is very unlikely that a company will go through the expense of uninstalling that system and switching to a different ERP system.

The same goes for making a commitment to build company computing and communications infrastructure. Once the technology from a given vendor or small group of vendors has been installed, it would require a great effort to switch to the technology of different vendors.

Over time, it may actually be easier to switch from one cloud provider to another than it is to switch from one software vendor to another for an in-house system. That's because clouds by definition are able to create virtual computers that you use to run your applications. As long as the operating system used by the virtual computers of one cloud provider is the same as the operating system used by another cloud provider, then it is possible to move the program code from one provider to another—and expect that application system to work going forward. Many cloud providers use a version of the Linux operating system, while others use Microsoft's Windows operating system.

Moving data is a final major consideration when thinking about moving your application system to a different cloud provider. Providers like Google and others are endorsing open standards (like HTML 5.0) that make it easier to move data from the database of one provider to that of another. These same data transfer standards are also making it easier to move large amounts of data back and forth between in-house systems and cloud systems.

Cloud Cost Considerations

To analyze a move to the cloud, the cost of using cloud systems is often compared to the cost of buying and operating the system hardware and software in-house. The answers generated in the comparison often depend on the depth of the analysis. On one level, a company can simply identify the rate for renting the use of a virtual server from a cloud provider and compare that with the cost of buying a real server. In that case, after a certain number of months, it might appear cheaper for a company to own and operate that server in-house. Therefore, if the application system it will power is expected to be used longer than that certain number of months, it might seem better to build and operate the system in-house instead of deploying it in the cloud.

A senior enterprise architect, Rick Pittard, a senior enterprise architect at a global 100 corporation, has been investigating this issue and working with some cloud-based applications to better understand this analysis. His observation with the cloud provider he uses is, "Hardware costs for short-term projects, up to two years, are less expensive than purchasing and operating our own. Systems that will operate for longer than two years may be more cost effective to operate in-house." He goes on to add, "but at three years you are getting close to replacement of the equipment and if you go through the replacement cycle to upgrade your hardware then there is no cost advantage to running it in-house. You might as well use a cloud provider instead."

People often forget to add all the indirect costs that go along with purchasing, installing, and operating their own computer equipment. Those costs add up to much more than the purchase price of the hardware. In their cost analysis companies need to include all of the related costs including:

- *People and electricity.* What is the cost of the people in procurement who negotiate purchase prices and support contracts? What are the costs of the people in IT who operate the equipment? What are the costs of the electricity, air conditioning, rent, and operation of the data center where this equipment is located?
- *System administration and asset tracking.* What is the cost of the people who maintain the system databases and do the system upgrades? What is the cost of the people who manage the software licenses and hardware leases and who then dispose of these assets at the end of their useful lifespan?
- *The opportunity cost of not doing other things with the money spent on the above.* Are there other places where you could use that money for better return? About 70 percent of most corporate IT budgets go to maintenance of existing systems and infrastructure. By using cloud services, a company might reduce

this percentage and spend their money on things that produce a higher return.

Yet none of these key points even consider what may be the biggest cost of all: senior management's time. If IT and operations management spend most of their time on operations staffing, data center build-out, and equipment leasing and installation, is that a good use of highly paid management time? It might be better spent on figuring out how to apply technology to sell more of the company's products, reduce operating expenses, and finding ways to use IT for competitive business advantage.

Case Study: Selling "Designer Chocolates"

In this business case, a company makes some well-known chocolate candies and sells them through a variety of retail channels. While it sells a substantial volume of candy nationwide, profit margins on candy are squeezed. Smart marketing people in the company spotted a business opportunity to sell "designer chocolates," cookies, and drinks through cozy storefront locations in upscale neighborhoods. The company won't sell as much volume of new product in these new venues as they do through traditional channels, but it will get a much higher profit margin on what it does sell. It's an opportunity for the company to supplement its traditional business with a new business that can generate big profits for an unknown and hard to predict period of time.

What would you do if you were the CIO or the COO of this company and you were asked how you would support this new designer chocolate business? Not many years ago, you'd require capital to create a dedicated IT infrastructure, or you would need to reassign corporate IT resources and development time to create systems to support the new venture. Today, technology has advanced such that you can create an agile IT architecture and leverage it to quickly support this new business venture. Imagine that Figure 5.1 shows what your existing infrastructure looks like. It was created over the years to support your traditional manufacturing business.

The key to meeting the company's needs for launching the new business is to leverage existing systems as much as possible in order to hold down costs and speed up delivery times for new systems. You could use server virtualization to better utilize existing servers and

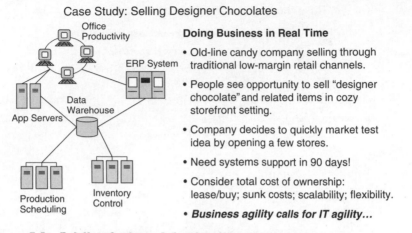

Case Study: Selling Designer Chocolates

Doing Business in Real Time

- Old-line candy company selling through traditional low-margin retail channels.

- People see opportunity to sell "designer chocolate" and related items in cozy storefront setting.

- Company decides to quickly market test idea by opening a few stores.

- Need systems support in 90 days!

- Consider total cost of ownership: lease/buy; sunk costs; scalability; flexibility.

- *Business agility calls for IT agility...*

Figure 5.1 Existing Systems Infrastructure

avoid having to buy any new hardware. And you could quickly implement a simple, open source, bare-bones retail point-of-sale system to support basic store operations.

You could set up a simple network using IaaS for each store to connect cash registers and PCs to the Internet. Using that connection and employing agile IT system development methods, you could use SOA to hook in functionality from the existing inventory control system to manage store inventories, and use the existing ERP system to handle accounting and financial reporting. A new supply chain database (a data warehouse) could be created using PaaS to store and report on all the business transactions related to store operations. This would provide the data needed to learn and continually adjust and improve operating processes of the new business. Figure 5.2 illustrates this approach.

In this case, you quickly deliver the first version of the Store Support System that's required to open a few stores and test the new business model. Let's then say that the concept is taking off. Business is good, and now the folks in marketing and sales want to open up more stores and add new features and products to the business model. Once again, you are asked to deliver the system capabilities needed to make the expansion possible. But no one knows just how far this expansion will go or how long this business will last.

How would you use agile IT architecture to keep supporting the growth of this business? Given the uncertainty of the venture, it's

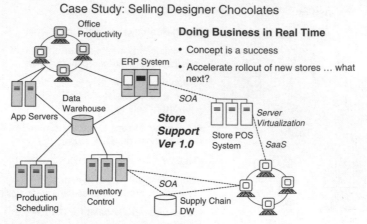

Figure 5.2   Extending Existing Infrastructure to Support a New Business

probably not wise to buy more servers to support more stores because you'd have to take on the cost and the risk of building up your data center, adding more system backup capability, and hiring more staff. Alternatively, you could use a cloud services provider to deliver all the computing power for the stores on a pay-as-you-go basis. This leaves you free to cut back on computing services if the business were to take an unexpected turn and not grow as expected.

As the overall business portfolio changed, you could also combine the needs of the new business with those of the existing business and look at retiring older IT architecture in favor of using more cloud computing models to meet changing company needs. This would turn fixed operating costs into variable costs and reduce the need for capital to purchase IT infrastructure. Operating costs would rise a bit as business grew, but operating costs would also drop if the business did not grow as expected, thus better protecting cash flow. The company would then not have to incur the risk of a big investment in IT infrastructure if the business is going through significant changes and long-term needs are hard to project. Figure 5.3 illustrates this approach.

These diagrams illustrate how many companies will be evolving their systems architecture in the coming years. Using these techniques and technologies enables companies to move quickly yet also minimize their investment risk in case a new business doesn't pan out, or shows promise but is unpredictable.

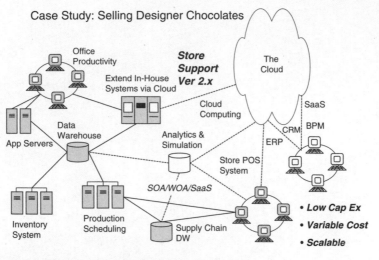

Figure 5.3 Moving New Systems to the Cloud as New Business Grows

These approaches are stable and scalable. They enable an organization to move quickly. Ready or not, *this is what the future of responsive IT infrastructure looks like.*

Notes

1. Joseph A. Schumpeter, *Capitalism, Socialism and Democracy* (New York: Harper, 1975) [orig. pub. 1942], pp. 82–85.
2. Bernard Golden, "The Case against Cloud Computing," CIO.com (January 22, 2009), www.cio.com/article/477473/The_Case_Against_Cloud_Computing_Part_One. In this popular five-part article Bernard Golden delivers an in-depth exploration of five major issues related to the adoption of cloud computing in business.
3. Bernard Golden, "McKinsey Cloud Computing Report Conclusions Don't Add Up," CIO.com (April 27, 2009), www.cio.com/article/490770/McKinsey_Cloud_Computing_Report_Conclusions_Don_t_Add_Up.
4. Rick Pittard, Chicago, comment made in telephone interview with authors (February 10, 2010).

The Transition from Managing Technology to Managing Business Processes

Technology does not generate revenue for most companies. Business processes powered by technology generate revenue and profits. The management of technology has just been a means to enable the operation of business processes. Cloud computing enables companies to make the shift from managing technology to managing business processes. And in the process of making that shift, companies can reduce their fixed cost structure and redirect their money to activities more directly related to generating revenue.

Tens of thousands of companies rely on one or more data centers to power the vast majority of their technology applications and transactions. Planning and constructing these data centers requires a capital expenditure that can reach into hundreds of millions of dollars, which doesn't include the ongoing operating expenses related to staffing, maintaining, and upgrading them.

The world's corporations have collectively built tens of thousands of data centers all replicating some basic functions, all providing the same capabilities, and all of them with considerable excess capacity. Numerous studies show that, in most companies, only about six percent of the total computing power in their data centers is ever in use at any given time.[1] The remaining additional power is there to handle occasional surges in demand or is simply there because it accumulated over time and no one did anything to stop it.

The Fixed Cost of Maintaining Large Data Centers Is Being Challenged

All of this duplicated processing power, like electricity, is a commodity, and leasing capacity from IT service providers will increasingly become a more attractive financial option to most organizations. A group of IT vendors are now in the business of selling computing power, data storage, and application systems to other companies on a pay-as-you-go basis. They are utilities for companies that want to pay for basic IT services as they need them, rather than incurring the high fixed costs of the traditional in-house IT operations model.

How many line-of-business professionals go through an entire day with either no IT service interruptions (or if they have any, they file a help-desk ticket to resolve an IT issue)—all without speaking directly to anyone in IT? IT has gotten so good at managing traditional IT services that for the larger business population that they can (and do) take IT for granted. IT services are ubiquitous. Internet access is ubiquitous. Access to key databases is ubiquitous. Access to IT support is readily available. Generally, these functions are becoming commoditized, and the most basic functions of IT by themselves are no longer part of the value proposition for most companies.

What would happen if it was quick and relatively easy (at least easier than the painful and lengthy process we have endured for the past 20 years) to develop new application systems? What if companies didn't need to buy new hardware or new packaged software, and then consume months or years to install those systems and then test and debug them and get them into production? What if new systems were rolled out in a few weeks or months and were constantly enhanced with new features as needs arose? Would this create a whole new level of opportunity to evolve and change your operations and products in order to keep up with the constantly changing wants and needs of your customers? How long will your company be able to survive without this ability?

Today, corporate IT groups spend 70 to 80 percent of their annual budgets on the operation and upkeep of data centers and standard application systems like enterprise resource planning (ERP), customer relationship management (CRM), and other commonly packaged applications. For the most part these activities don't provide meaningful differentiation in the marketplace, nor do they provide a competitive advantage. By using cloud technologies to provide more of these basic services, companies have the opportunity to shift more of their annual IT budgets to spending on new systems and capabilities that will more directly relate to the success and growth of their business.

Cloud computing gives companies a way to both reduce costs and improve service. Cloud computing is an opportunity to standardize the basic computing and communications infrastructure a company employs, and this standardization offers the prospect of getting systems built and into production in a much more agile manner than ever before. And this agile use of IT can be a potent factor in driving business agility. When companies can try out new product ideas and explore new markets without incurring large up-front capital expenses, then many more opportunities open up.

Public, Private, and Hybrid Clouds

Despite the debates about the exact definition of cloud computing, it's generally agreed that the cloud computing model has a handful of common characteristics:

- Massive scalability
- Provisioning of computing resources on demand
- A pay-as-you-go cost structure
- Multiple systems and multiple users supported on the same computing infrastructure
- Systems and data available from anywhere with Internet connectivity; built-in disaster recovery
- Software that's focused on ease of use for the customer

Within this broad vision of cloud computing we can then provide three basic models of cloud computing:

1. *Public clouds* are owned and operated by third parties and located in data centers that operate outside of the companies that use them. Multiple companies share these resources; they are each assigned their own virtual computing capabilities based on a common set of physical resources. Public clouds are provided by companies like Amazon, Hewlett-Packard, IBM, Google, Microsoft, Rackspace, and Salesforce.com.

2. *Private clouds* are owned and operated by a company or a cloud computing provider, but they are built for the sole use of a single company. Private clouds utilize the same technology as public clouds and they are often built to enable an individual company to maximize the use of its computing resources and be more responsive to company needs than was possible under the traditional IT operating model.

3. *Hybrid clouds* are combinations of multiple clouds that are both public and private. These clouds are created by individual customers to meet their specific needs. For example, a company may decide to create a hybrid cloud to combine a CRM system provided on a public cloud operated by Sales-Force.com with an ERP system running on their private cloud, and they may further extend this hybrid cloud by combining it with the Google cloud in order to provide their employees with the collaboration and productivity tools provided by Google Apps. These hybrid clouds sometimes rely on the services of a cloud aggregator.

Up to this point, we have focused our discussion on the use of public clouds and the business reasons for doing so. For many start-up companies, it makes sense to start immediately with the use of a public cloud instead of investing precious capital in building their own data centers. By doing this, they avoid the distractions of running commodity computer hardware and software and are able to concentrate on developing their unique value-added product or service that will be the profit generator for the company.

But for existing companies that have already made significant investments over many years in creating and running in-house systems infrastructure, the choice of how to proceed with the use of cloud technology is not as clear. They can consider the choices of creating private clouds or deploying hybrid clouds.

Private Clouds

Many industry analysts believe that private clouds (as opposed to public clouds) will remain attractive to in-house IT groups for the foreseeable future since they can offset concerns about governance, data security, and performance management.[2] Private clouds also offer large companies an inviting way to consolidate data centers, cut technical support and operations staff, and increase server utilization. Typical server utilization inside corporate data centers ranges from as low as 2 percent up to around 10 percent. Implementing a private cloud can raise those levels to 60 or 70 percent and save the company from purchasing a lot of additional servers.[3]

In addition, private clouds don't need to be quite as automated and self-serve as public clouds in order for them to still deliver value with increased server utilization and faster user provisioning. Instead of using online web request forms to provision computing services for a new application system, employees could just send an email to their IT provisioning group with the request. The in-house IT group could get it done and email the requestor back in a few hours with the confirmation and information they need to start using the newly provisioned system.

Larger companies enjoy economies of scale in IT operations and, in some cases, can provide IaaS (infrustructure-as-a-service) and PaaS (platform-as-a-service) less expensively than services from outside cloud providers. For certain categories of services, private clouds can make good business sense.

Private clouds may not need to run entirely on uniform hardware in the same way public clouds do. For instance, IBM has experience building private clouds that use products like Tivoli on its mainframes, Windows and Linux on its servers, and Websphere transaction management and SOA (service-oriented architecture) as well as MQ Series for message sharing among these different platforms. By configuring this way, they are able to create fit-for-purpose clouds and increase the utilization of each platform.

Based on the specific circumstances and business conditions for a particular company, building a private cloud in the typical corporate heterogeneous environment offers advantages including:

- Enabling IT organizations to leverage existing infrastructure and get cost-effective use of their previous IT investments.
- Placing cloud computing inside the corporate data center to eliminate many of the issues that accompany the use of public clouds like data security; performance management and SLAs; and concerns about regulatory compliance.
- Private clouds also have the potential of lower cost of use, since they don't have a profit margin added onto their services (as is the case with public clouds).

Until companies are familiar with this new operating model, some may feel that external cloud environments have too many unknowns and too much risk. In building their private clouds, companies can gradually invest in their private cloud as the first step on a journey to get more comfortable with a cloud operating model. Private clouds are a good way to test maturity and reliability of the technology. Companies can develop trust in the technology and the pubic cloud providers they do work with on a limited scale, and they can learn to deal with different regulatory, data control, and security issues.

Then, over time the in-house private cloud versus public cloud mix can evolve from 90-10 to a 50-50 mix or even a 20-80 mix. That said, large companies may not get to an all-or-nothing, public-versus-private cloud model any time soon.

Hybrid Clouds

A company may create a private cloud to share IT resources across multiple applications and to increase utilization of the servers in their data center. Suppose that company starts to experience a surge in user demand for one of their applications. By using a hybrid cloud, they can quickly and cost effectively expand the capacity of the servers in their private cloud. They can draw upon the power of a public cloud to handle the increased user demand and maintain good system service levels for the people using it.

To create a hybrid cloud, companies need to put the infrastructure in place that will allow them to integrate public clouds with their private clouds while still maintaining security and performance management capabilities. IT vendor companies (like Cisco, Itricity, Juniper Networks, and Nimsoft) are making the technology that allows companies to do this. This is the underlying infrastructure companies need for hybrid clouds.

Integration of cloud applications and in-house systems requires an effective method for maintaining security, for monitoring performance, and for passing data back and forth between the cloud and the in-house systems. Perimeter security in hybrid clouds can be provided by a number of methods like data encryption and virtual private networks. Many in-house IT groups are already familiar with the use of this technology.

Most cloud vendors provide robust tools to help manage system performance in the cloud. This is the business they are in so they invest heavily in performance monitoring and reporting capabilities that are often superior to what companies have in-house. Once in place, this infrastructure becomes the base for new business models. It allows rapid expansion and contraction of computing power as business needs change, and it also provides the security, performance management, and regulatory compliance needed to operate hybrid clouds.

Cloud applications are by their nature relatively easy to integrate with other systems because they are built with well-defined application interfaces known as application programming interfaces (APIs). Compared with the task of integrating different in-house applications, integrating cloud applications with in-house applications is often easier because the APIs of cloud applications make it easier to import and export data and pass that data back and forth between the cloud and in-house systems.

Issues to Consider with Private Clouds

Private clouds encounter all the same issues associated with public clouds and they require significant up-front capital investment. They have the same problems with monitoring and managing performance. They have the same problems with the risk of vendor lock-in (particularly with respect to the virtualization technology used)[4] and the question of whether that vendor will keep up with the pace of technology change in the marketplace.

Private clouds present a significant challenge for internal IT groups because they often have not dealt with the required business process reengineering steps and processes. ITIL (information technology infrastructure library) is a popular set of best practices that are widely used to run the in-house data centers of individual companies. In turn, ITIL practices are going to clash with cloud practices because ITIL is very manually intensive and clouds, by definition, must be highly automated in order to achieve the levels of user self-service and the rapid infrastructure provisioning required for meeting user service requests.

At present there are relatively few in-house IT groups that can match the operating discipline, the automation, and the resultant efficiencies of the big cloud data centers operated by providers like Amazon, Google, IBM, Microsoft, and Rackspace. Cloud vendors invest in their infrastructure and in automated systems administration capabilities in order to achieve great economies of scale and operating efficiency. Conversely, in-house IT groups are always being squeezed to save money and to cut their operations budgets so they are challenged to create the economies of scale that public cloud vendors can achieve.

As Irving Wladawsky-Berger puts it, most company data centers are a hodge-podge of different technology reflecting the company's history with different vendors and its mergers and acquisitions.[5] He points out that they look like what most factories looked like before the advent of lean manufacturing practices. The engineering disciplines promoted by lean manufacturing and implemented by the Japanese and Germans have set a standard that every other manufacturing company needs to match if they want to achieve world-class productivity and cost efficiency levels. Companies need to adopt similar practices and discipline with the equipment, layout, and operation of their data centers.

Public cloud vendors are bringing this same discipline to bear on their cloud data centers. The public cloud vendors have implemented a new world-class level of practices and use of equipment that in-house IT groups must also adopt if they want to achieve the same level of productivity and efficiency.

Based on his experience over the last couple of years, senior enterprise architect Rick Pittard puts it this way; he says, "Size of data centers is important but may not be as central to gaining economies of scale as having a standardized hardware and operating system environment. Size and standardization are both necessary to get real economies of scale. If you have size, it can reduce cost if you also have standardization, but without standardization, size alone will not reduce your costs. Without standards, the diversity of hardware makes it very hard to move into a cloud environment."[6]

Cloud computing by its nature requires a lot of innovation. It demands steady innovation to make it work and to make it easy to use by a mass consumer market. Public cloud vendors in the business-to-consumer world have innovated rapidly and done so over the last several years in spite of our difficult economic situation. At the same time, where in the corporate IT world has so much changed in so short a time? The innovation cycles of public cloud vendors are usually much shorter than most corporate IT life cycles; most companies work on five to six year life cycles or longer. It will be a challenge for corporate IT environments to keep up with the pace of change initiated by public cloud vendors.

The rapid innovation cycles of public cloud providers like Google and Amazon are driven by real-time customer feedback loops. That customer feedback drives their innovation in a much more effective manner than the feedback that drives traditional IT vendors and in-house IT groups largely because the central business of cloud service providers is to make money by responding quickly to customer needs. In-house IT groups don't have that same, dynamic incentive and are not seen as profit centers in their companies so they do not have access to the same levels of investment to improve their service offerings.

Private clouds, if not used carefully, can defeat the central purpose and the value proposition that clouds provide to companies because with private clouds, companies still have the distraction of buying servers, building data centers, operating them, and so on. In-house IT staff is still focused on running existing technology and systems instead of figuring out what new tools and infrastructure the company needs.

The Cloud Is a Platform for Managing Business Processes

In our real-time, global economy where product life cycles are short, companies need to be good at bringing new products to market and tailoring existing products to keep up with shifting customer preferences. In their ongoing search for new products and new markets, companies engage in growth by expansion of existing business units and by mergers and acquisitions of other companies. Business processes need to be flexible to accommodate these activities.

The value proposition delivered by most companies (unless they are themselves cloud service providers) lies in the way they manage their business processes, not their technology. It lies in the way they tailor their processes to meet constantly changing market conditions. Technology is a means to this end, but technology is not an end in itself.

Although the cloud is certainly a platform for managing the delivery of computing services, that view is more from the traditional technology-oriented perspective. Another way to look at the cloud is from the business perspective of companies that use the cloud to support their operations. From their point of view, the greatest benefit they can gain from the cloud comes not from cost savings in technology, but from the revenue they earn by being more responsive to changing customer needs, the revenue they generate with faster roll out of new products and services, and successful expansion into new markets.

In addition, it's important to remember that companies are much less self-contained and much less vertically integrated than they were 20 years ago. Companies have been steadily outsourcing noncore activities so that they can concentrate their time and money on conducting the value-added activities that create the product or service their customers buy from them. As a consequence, most companies are dependent on a network of suppliers that provide support services. And for companies to manage their business processes effectively, they need to find ways to effectively collaborate with their supplier partners. Figure 6.1 illustrates these interconnections that are now the norm for most companies.

The cloud is not so much about new technology as it is about new business models. The business model in Figure 6.1 shows how companies are evolving away from self-contained organizations that perform all their core and support activities internally. Companies

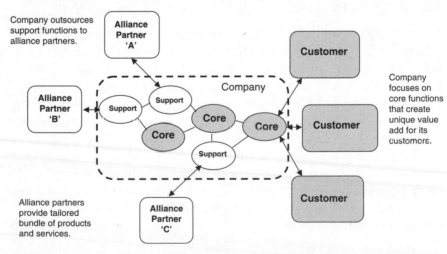

Figure 6.1   Companies Are Dependent on an Ecosystem of Suppliers and Customers

are now becoming enmeshed in networks of suppliers and customers. To paraphrase a famous saying, no company is an island. No company can succeed all by itself. Companies depend more than ever on effective collaboration with their supplier partners. Business services need to be delivered in a reliable and predictable fashion, and it is the flow of information back and forth between companies through the cloud that makes this possible.

The cloud is an ideal environment for companies to build and deliver an inventory of business services targeted to individual market segments and specific customers. Business process management (BPM) is the foundation for offering business services over the cloud. Using BPM, companies working together can assemble an appropriate bundle of business services needed to best serve certain kinds of customers. BPM systems can then monitor performance of these intercompany services and provide all parties with the real-time reporting and transparency they need so as to continually adjust the business processes that deliver these services as conditions change.

BPM systems tap into and monitor the data that flows between the transaction processing systems used by companies. For instance, consider a business process that involves receiving orders, that then routes the orders for fulfillment, ships the ordered products, and then bills the customer. There are several transaction processing systems involved: a web-based product catalog and order-entry system; an order-routing system; an order-fulfillment system; a billing system; and an accounts receivable system. To really understand what is happening in the process, and to optimize the whole process of taking orders and serving the customer, you need to see and understand how all these systems work together. A BPM system can reveal a unified, big-picture view of the data flowing between these systems, and it can spot bottlenecks where data flow slows down or where problems develop that place a drag on efficiency throughout the whole process.

A recent report from Gartner states, "By 2013 dynamic BPM will be an imperative for companies seeking process efficiencies in increasingly chaotic environments."[7] It also says that more and more customer-facing processes will be configured based on specific knowledge about the customer, and suppliers will use BPM to tailor their processes on a just-in-time basis to meet the evolving needs of customers.

In other words, BPM systems deployed in a cloud environment then become the method companies will work together in value chains to deliver a constantly changing mix of responsive products and services to their customers. As a result, cloud-based BPM then becomes the basis for effective, cross-company collaboration to deliver personalized and specialized processes that support individual customers.

BPM and SOA are two different sides of the same coin. BPM is the business view and SOA is the technology view. BPM allows companies to model their business processes, and then combine and streamline them. SOA allows companies to reuse software assets and cost-effectively create systems to support redesigned business process flows. Companies can use SOA or WOA (web-oriented architecture) to integrate across different clouds and integrate cloud applications with internal company systems.

BPM allows companies to break their business processes into collections of interconnected tasks. This is an important step in enabling them to extend their operations beyond their own company boundaries to embrace services provided over the cloud. In this way, they can outsource certain processes and tasks so that they can concentrate on their core value-added processes, continue to improve them, and invent new ones.

In a world where products and services quickly become commodities and where profit margins are constantly being squeezed as a result, it's the ability to continuously tailor these products and services that will earn companies an additional profit margin on top of the diminishing margins offered by those otherwise commodity products.

The driving force of the responsive economy in this century is coming from unleashed innovation through cloud services that are quickly becoming available all over the world. Scientists can collaborate on health and environmental problems; businesses can cooperate to deliver tailored products and services worldwide; and in these business networks, companies can focus on doing what they do best and rely on other companies to perform the complementary tasks that are a part of delivering the finished product to the end-user customer.

It is in this agile process of continuous response to changing customer needs that most companies will differentiate themselves and find most of their profit opportunities. These profits are the "agility dividend." Real-time, global markets are continuously adjusting the price of commodity products to their cost of production just as real-time stock markets continually adjust the price of stocks. So the agility dividend is where most companies will find their best opportunities to generate profitable revenue over and above the prices set by global markets.

Automate Routine Processes and Focus People on Handling Exceptions

Companies are like fish swimming in oceans of data. There is just not enough time or budget for all those people to handle or review standard information recorded as predictable, expected operations taking place in a company. Routine, standard data, and procedures for handling it, must be driven by automated transaction systems that support the company's standard operating procedures. Computers handle routine situations much better than humans because they never get bored by the routine, and they scale up quickly as transaction volumes increase.

People in a responsive organization need to devote their time to handling nonstandard data. Nonstandard data is any kind of data that is different from what is expected: data that, for any reason, does not conform to the rules built into automated transaction systems or the performance parameters built into performance monitoring systems. When a company's systems encounter this kind of data, people quickly get involved. The greatest opportunities for any organization are in the way they detect and respond to unexpected problems, threats, or opportunities.

Use computers to do what they do best. Let them handle the day-in, day-out moving of routine data on basic transactions like purchase orders, invoices, account balances, order status, address changes, and so on. Wherever there are people doing routine data entry or repetitious work of any sort, this is an opportunity to automate. Computers do this sort of work much better, faster, and cheaper than people.

Use people to do what they do best. What they do best is thinking, communicating, and problem solving. We don't need to build excessive amounts of complexity and cost into new computer systems if we free people up from routine work, then give them the data and training they need to solve complex problems and the ability to handle the exceptions discovered by computers through automated, routine operations. We don't need artificial intelligence in our systems when we can apply the real intelligence of people who are trained, motivated, and empowered.

Most business operations are routine and repetitive work that can be handled with relatively simple sets of processing rules that can be applied to business processes with BPM systems. The BPM systems can be used to move and monitor data between different systems and different companies. They monitor the processes they support and when they detect a problem or a slow down, they send alerts to people assigned to handle those issues. Whenever a transaction happens that doesn't follow one of the simple routine processing rules, the BPM system traps the data related to that transaction and notifies a qualified person.

People will either be able to correct the data so that it fits back into a simple predefined process, or they will take care of the transactions themselves all the way through. They will have adequate time to do this since they won't be bogged down or worn out doing the routine work the computers handle. And this is where they can generate the most value for customers and for the company; this is the agility dividend.

And people will do a great job on these tasks. Since they are nonroutine, they are interesting. They involve thinking, communicating with others, and problem solving. People like this kind of work. It's fun. The human brain is more fine-tuned and able than any computer to do this kind of work.

By automating the mass of rote, routine, and repetitious work, your organization will find great cost efficiencies. By empowering people to handle the nonroutine tasks, companies will become very responsive to unique customer needs. It is this blend of efficiency and responsiveness that will enable a company to outperform its competition.

Cost savings happen when companies act in a coordinated manner to continually optimize their common and individual business processes, and then regularly adjust them to changing business conditions. These adjustments are made in response to changes in the cost of labor and raw materials as well as to supply and demand for a company's products and services.

Profits are generated by continuous tailoring of products and services to changing customer needs and desires. Products that are tailored to meet demanding customer service requirements are worth more than the commodity versions of those products. This tailoring results in sales revenue that is slightly higher than the market average because customers are willing to pay a few percent more to get those tailored products.

Four Technologies that Enable Responsive Business Processes

There are four application technologies that companies can use in various combinations to be responsive to changing conditions and emerging threats and opportunities. They are:

1. Business process management (BPM)
2. Complex event processing (CEP)
3. Business intelligence (BI)
4. Simulation modeling

BPM is a way for companies to observe productivity in their operations and carry out a continuous, incremental process of improving operational performance. A company starts by mapping out its key processes and defines the steps or work tasks in each process. Then it uses BPM software to collect and display a continuous stream of data that shows the movement of transactions through each step. The BPM software can be used to automate many of the routine tasks, such as moving different kinds of data from one task to another. It can also be set to detect certain error conditions and send automatic alerts to people who need to respond to these conditions quickly.

CEP complements the capabilities of BPM systems. A CEP system can monitor multiple data streams and can conduct real-time comparisons of data in these streams that predefined patterns indicating the occurrence of certain events that create problems or opportunities. Companies can define specific event patterns that then trigger the system to make certain responses. Some events may trigger the system to set in motion a set of online calculations and responses that react to those events. Other events may trigger the system to send alerts to people. For instance, a CEP system used by an airline might detect that a particular airplane is at a departure airport and that a large storm is heading to that geography. It also detects the boarding gate at the arrival airport reserved for that airplane. In these data streams, the system can be instructed to automatically detect that the airplane's departure will be delayed by the approaching storm and that the time slot reserved for the boarding gate at the arrival airport requires change. The system can be instructed to make the change itself, or it can send an alert to airline staff so they can respond appropriately.

BI systems collect, store, and analyze data and allow people to orient themselves to patterns and decide on actions to take. These systems collect data from many different sources. Data can be collected from sensors and radio-frequency identification (RFID) devices. Data can be collected by BPM systems or data can be obtained from the many transaction processing systems in a company like ERP, order entry, or CRM. Once the data is collected, it is stored in a database where people then access it as needed. Often the database is updated with new data on a continuous or "real-time" basis, and summary displays of relevant data are available to people through web-based dashboards.

When people then access the data, they use BI software tools that help them analyze the information and display the results. BI software tools run the gamut from simple spreadsheets and charts to complex multivariable regression analysis and linear programming. The proper mix of BI tools is determined by the needs of the people in a particular business setting, and their skill and training levels. The combination of BPM, CEP, and BI systems is sometimes referred to as enterprise performance management (EPM).

Simulation modeling is an emerging software category. Today, companies need to make important decisions more frequently, and these decisions have significant consequences on company operations and profitability. As well, they need to make decisions about how to operate in conditions they've sometimes never encountered. Simulation modeling provides a way to deal with this kind of rapid and business-critical decision making.

Simulation modeling software allows people to create models of scenarios like a factory or a supply chain network or a vehicle delivery route. They can then subject the models to different inputs and situations and observe what happens. A design that may seem good on paper could very well create problems that aren't apparent until the design is modeled and its performance is simulated under a broad range of conditions. It is much faster and cheaper to discover problems through simulations than to find out the hard way after much time and capital are invested.

Existing transaction systems, like ERP, order management, accounting, inventory management, delivery scheduling, factory control, and maintenance systems, provide a steady stream of data that reflects individual processes in a company or between groups of companies. This data can be monitored through the use of BPM and CEP systems to provide a comprehensive end-to-end picture of the productivity and performance levels in these operating processes. BPM systems can update this picture on a real-time or near-real-time basis and reveal bottlenecks and disruptions that require attention.

Once people have identified the snags, they can then make use of BI databases and analytics software to investigate the problems and identify their root causes. When these are revealed, people can design appropriate ways to address them. Then, by using simulation systems, they can model potential process changes and see the probable impact of each different change. In this way, people are then able to select the most effective changes and implement them with confidence that they will deliver the desired results.

The power of these four technologies is multiplied when they are used together and on a universally accessible platform like the cloud, largely because they enable more effective and timely collaboration among companies working together. When these technologies run in the cloud, people in all participating companies can see data and the status of operating processes in real time. This transparency enables effective and timely brainstorming as well as problem solving. In this environment, companies have the opportunity to collaborate and design extraordinarily responsive business processes to drive their operations and that enable them to continuously and instantly adjust their operations to *changing and unpredictable circumstances.*

Notes

1. Ludwig Siegele, "Where the Cloud Meets the Ground," *The Economist*, October 23, 2008.
2. Mark Everett Hall, "Pioneers of the Private Cloud," *Computerworld*, December 21, 2009, www.computerworld.com/s/article/345397/Pioneers_of_the_Private_Cloud.
3. Ibid.

4. Bernard Golden, "The Case against Private Clouds," CIO.com, June 4, 2009, www.cio.com/article/494249/The_Case_Against_Private_Clouds.
5. Irving Wladawsky-Berger, Somers, NY, comments made in personal interview with authors (December 16, 2009).
6. Rick Pittard, Chicago, comments made in telephone interview with authors (February 10, 2010).
7. Gartner, "Five Business Process Management Predictions for 2010 and Beyond," Gartner.com, January 13, 2010, www.gartner.com/it/page.jsp?id=1278415.

CHAPTER 7

The New Role of Information Technology

Nicholas Carr, a thoughtful, and controversial, observer of technology and its effect on business, asked if traditional IT was still relevant in his 2003 *Harvard Business Review* article titled, "IT Doesn't Matter." The article generated surprisingly great fanfare and strong reactions. The IT vendor community, as well as many CIOs, took great offense to this notion, largely since it suggested that IT, as it came to be known in the last couple of decades of the twentieth century, was a commodity service and didn't provide companies with a competitive advantage.

But the more contemporary question today might be, "Are traditional IT functions a core competency? Or should they best be entrusted to companies that specialize in delivering them to large customer bases?" Nicholas Carr eventually found momentum with his ideas and philosophies, many of which were updated and explained in his 2008 book, *The Big Switch: Rewiring the World, from Edison to Google.*[1]

Is Traditional IT Irrelevant?

In a discussion with Nicholas Carr in 2009 he talked about where he thinks the data center—and all the corporate staff needed to operate it—are headed. Here's some of what he had to say.

> What we know is that most people in corporate IT today are mechanics. They keep the stuff running—the machines, the

applications. And I think that all of the trends in the marketplace today point to a winnowing of the IT workforce. Not just because of the cloud computing option available to CIOs, but because of all kinds of economically driven consolidation opportunities with virtualization and more efficient technologies.

So what does this mean for the role of traditional IT departments? Once you get rid of managing the infrastructure, a lot of the budget and head count goes away. My own sense is that the IT function, which in the past has focused on IT as a business input, wasn't really directly influencing what you were selling anyway. And as companies begin to move away from running their own IT infrastructure, IT as a business output will then become more and more important. As we see more IT incorporated in more and more products and services, that's where the IT energy will be focused. And while the CIO and IT staff will still need to spend time purchasing services from the cloud, there will be an increasing emphasis on how the information flows *through* companies, rather than on the data center itself.

In smaller companies, it's very possible that the IT function and the CIO become less relevant. As the trends continue, a lot of what the CIO was responsible for there just goes away, and the rest will just filter into the existing business organization, which means that the raison d'être of the CIO—as we once knew it—just goes away.[2]

History has been suggesting this change for some time. Since the turn of the century, IT has become central to all business operations, but the importance of the traditional IT profession has declined. Unlike the 1980s, where information technology largely dealt with back-office and financial reporting applications, it now is embedded in every line of business in every function—from sales and marketing, to operations, to logistics, to manufacturing.

For many years now, IT has done far more than accounting and financial reporting. It is now integral to planning and operating any line of business operation. It predicts the best revenue management scenarios for individual properties within large hotel chains; it shows casinos how and where their highest-yield customers are spending their money; it optimizes the scheduling and routing of airlines to maximize operating profits. And the list of vitally important applications goes on.

So why, in the face of all of this line-of-business promise, is IT no longer at the center stage? To answer this, let's take a look at the recent fits and starts in the CIO's career.

A Tumultuous Ride for the Chief Information Officer

The title of Chief Information Officer caught momentum in the early 1980s and the role of people with that title has undergone significant changes ever since. In the early days, those who were appointed to such important posts found themselves under unrealistic pressure. In fact, their tenures in the early days were so short—perhaps only two years at a stint at best—that the media began to say that CIO stood for career-is-over. Then, through the 1990s as computer technology became steadily more powerful and more important to business operations, CIO success stories began to proliferate, as did the reputation of the position.

There were many reasons the CIO was gaining in business stature. First, technologies were enabling far more than just back-office applications, and some industries were realizing market advantages by making information technology more than just a back-office enabler. Second, CIOs were increasingly being recognized for their efforts, and some were even darlings of business change. In a few industries, like financial services where the speed and latency of massively used IT applications directly affects the bottom line, CIOs who could manage such challenges across a global infrastructure were drawing seven-figure salaries. And third, there was a never-ending need to close the gap between the needs of the business and the geeky technologists. All of these things made the CIO's role more popular.

The promise of the Internet then pushed the CIO squarely into the business spotlight they had been eyeing for years. Ultimately, as more corporations created a Web presence and began to conduct Internet-enabled business in more efficient and direct ways, IT budgets and related responsibility blossomed. The need to be part of Internet success was raging within all companies. Investments were questioned with less scrutiny, and the technology start-ups and providers that enabled Internet presence were succeeding beyond even their own expectations.

But it was short-lived. The market determined that the mere promise of more and more revenue from Internet channels wasn't enough. Revenue and profits from user corporations had to be realized, and cavalier bets came to a screeching halt starting in 2000. Many remember the high-profile fall of Internet start-up Toysmart.com. It was just one of thousands of start-ups, but it unfortunately was one that happened to be particularly well-funded by Disney, and Disney had had enough—enough of the promise. And it abruptly halted funding and suspended operations. From there, the cascade of promising start-ups with suspended funding began to accelerate. The ensuing dot-com bust was a painful correction that left many CIOs either out of work or working for the CFO instead of the CEO. Ever since then, CIOs across the corporate landscape have struggled in varying degrees to rise to boardroom status. Some have it. Some don't. And it's often directly related to the company's philosophy of IT as a cost center or as a strategic business investment.

The End of IT as We Know It

Traditional computing models are changing as you read this. They're morphing directly under the feet of the chief information officer, and the CIO's teams will remain in specific companies only to the extent that their activities contribute directly to increased profitability, sales growth, and development of new products and services. In today's climate, there is no longer room for operational luxuries, empires, traditions, and "we've always done it this way."

As a result, IT operations that are simply cost centers with support activities are being outsourced. Since these operations are no longer competitive differentiators, there is an inexorable economic drive for most companies to delegate this work to a smaller group of service providers that specialize in getting it done better than the in-house team largely because the providers can deliver higher levels of service at lower costs than if companies continue to operate them internally.

So what will the evolving internal company IT groups look like? They are teams of high-performing, technology-savvy, and business-smart people who embed themselves directly in the business operating units they support. Their value will come from their ability to proactively deliver the information systems that their business units need to achieve their profit objectives. As business conditions change, as new business opportunities arise, and as urgent needs emerge for effective and timely delivery of new systems to support new business, CIOs and their teams will increasingly be expected to respond without distractions created by operational issues.

Changes in IT and Business Unit Staffing

There is a great divide in the IT business between people who deliver services based on their knowledge of IT products, and people who deliver services based on their knowledge of the core IT techniques, largely since IT is actually reaching a new level of maturity. Up until about 1980, technology didn't change that quickly, and practitioners tended to identify themselves by the programming language, operating system, or hardware they knew.

The pace of change accelerated in the client/server world of the 1990s. Popular languages came and went every three or four years. (Remember dBase and PowerBuilder?) Hardware and operating systems got better and more powerful every year.

This forced people to take one of two paths. The first was to devote themselves full time to learning new languages and staying current with the newest release of an operating system. The other was to learn to apply a set of techniques that could be employed in a range of business situations regardless of the specific technology being used.

Since hardware and software vendors are consolidating rapidly, there are only a few dominant software packages, operating systems, and hardware platforms left. Use of an ERP (enterprise resource planning), CRM (customer relationship management), or office automation system no longer creates a competitive skill advantage as it once did. The installation and operation of these systems by a few large service providers—cloud service utilities—is rapidly becoming a very cost-effective way to go. Organizations are reaching a point where they no longer need to have people skilled in operating such systems on their own payrolls.

IT practitioners whose skills are largely based on detailed knowledge of a certain software package, programming language, or operating system are heading for a future in a cloud services utility or a SaaS (software-as-a-service) vendor company. Practitioners who apply a set of core techniques to design and build systems enabling organizations to accomplish their unique goals are the ones who will define the future of the IT profession. These practitioners will be indispensable to the way organizations deliver products and services to their customers.

Precisely because software packages are so common, the level of competition is increasing and the opportunities for growth and profit are shifting to new areas. Profit no longer lies in pumping out masses of commodity products to as large an audience as possible. Profit now lies in wrapping commodity products in a blanket of customized, value-added services that make them uniquely attractive to each customer. And since all value-added services are information-based, companies urgently need IT professionals who know how to use technology to deliver this value.

Evolution of the Traditional Corporate IT Department

Rick Pittard, an Enterprise Architect in a Global 100 energy company, made this assessment when he looked at the changes happening to in-house IT groups, "I find a lack of understanding on the part of many traditional IT folks of the changes in the marketplace. They don't see themselves as providing a service that could be provided by various marketplace options; they see themselves as running a data center in which they are heavily invested."[3]

"People focused on building and operating data centers often don't realize how much things have changed in the last few years. When they hear of new offerings from cloud vendors, their attitude is 'we can do that too. . . .' But for us to do that in a cost-effective business sense we would have to provide significant capital investment to do it, and companies are reluctant to do this now."

Many IT groups are developing agendas to move from builders of IT assets to providers of business solutions. They are looking to transition away from spending 70 percent of their time on maintenance and operations of nondifferentiator systems. This trend will also lead to a diminishing demand for traditional in-house IT staff whose primary jobs are to install and operate IT infrastructure such as servers and routers and private communications networks. But there will be other needs generated by the use of cloud-based systems that these people can be redeployed to address.

Traditional data center operations skills will still be needed, to some lesser degree, to watch over the evolving hybrid systems infrastructure. IT enterprise architects will still be needed in-house to design and direct evolution of the infrastructure. There will also be new needs to integrate in-house legacy applications like ERP systems with the new cloud-specific applications. In addition, there will be a need to address the security issues that arise from this new systems architecture. And there will remain a need to monitor and manage the overall network performance created by the integration of in-house and cloud systems.

Smart IT groups will not resist this new business dynamic. They will instead help their business units evaluate and select the right SaaS and cloud computing capabilities. This will lead to a growth in the demand for companies to have more in-house business analysts and enterprise architects.

The IT talent that companies need to keep and grow is their ability to be responsive to their customers and markets. Technology groups that remain within companies will change their focus from data center operations to the design, construction, and constant adjustment of systems that meet ever-changing business conditions. The value of IT groups within most companies will no longer be measured by how well they operate information technology but by how well they combine technology with business processes to create a stream of responsive and profitable products and services for their companies and customers.

Enterprise architects and business analysts will be embedded in line-of-business units, and they will be responsible for working with the businesspeople to design needed systems and oversee development of those systems. Development of new systems will be done by a mix of in-house developers working with outside consulting firms that bring special expertise to a specific application or technology need.

Agile IT Professionals Using Cloud Technology Will be Embedded in Business Operating Units

According to Yuri Aguiar, Senior Partner and Chief Information Officer at global advertising giant Ogilvy Worldwide, technology is high on the list of priorities among today's business leaders.[4] Savvy CEOs are intensely interested in knowing not only how technology can enhance their products and services, but how newer technology organizations or departments will be built inside today's companies.

Not surprisingly, these CEOs are looking for people to lead these organizations who are capable of understanding both sides of the coin: not just the technology side, but innovative ways to weave technology into the business.

In Yuri's case, the CEO wants his top technologist reporting directly to him and the CFO—and wants him on the company's worldwide executive board. The last time we saw this trend was during the Internet bubble (but when the bubble burst, many CIOs were relegated to reporting only to the cost-controlling CFO). But as technology is appearing in more and more product offerings of mainstream businesses, many CEOs want their top technologist working directly for them. And unlike previous generations where the CIO might have lobbied for this reporting relationship, the CEO is now asking for it. For his part, Yuri feels fortunate to be working in an organization where a forward-thinking board of directors gives an empowered technology department the freedom to build business-oriented technology solutions.

Yuri needs that kind of backing. The challenges in today's business world are complex enough, so when you add the demands to support technology for globally diverse clients, the degree of difficulty rises exponentially. For example, Yuri's team can find themselves creating and supporting applications for global brands across locations ranging from the United Kingdom to the Czech Republic to South Africa. Imagine one client, found in many locations around the world with different cultures, business conditions, languages, customs, and time zones. In cases like these, he needs technology experts savvy enough to take a step back, then assess how best to create a new delivery model for the client, and ultimately identify how to best apply technology to facilitate the business process. This is forcing a redefinition of the technology department. Moreover, "service level" and "service delivery" mean something different than they did just a few years ago.

For Yuri, there is a clear distinction between processing power and information. According to Yuri:

> A good information system gives you data. Turning that data into information we can act on is what's important. No one is interested these days in how many CPUs you have. Users (and the people who build business applications and solutions) are interested in getting at the information they need.

We're moving away from the geeky way technology works, and instead are bringing in the technologists who understand what the business needs to do. That's a complete departure from the previous generation of CIOs who wanted to be associated with a significant ERP implementation, or to deliver the best networking, or the fastest computers. Today, we have to assume that all of the back-office computing is a given. We shouldn't be thinking about specifications for SAP equipment. That sort of thing should be on autopilot, and it shouldn't be the cornerstone of discussion.

Not surprisingly, futurist Paul Saffo agrees. He thinks IT talent will increasingly come from people who are building webs and working more in the service-oriented space. "In periods of rapid change, people responsible for IT need to go deeper into the issues of the company. The systems are going deeper into the organization, so the IT organization has to follow them deeper into the company." Paul points out that IT professionals are being pushed more and more to the outer edge of the company—closer to customers and closer to people to support customers.

Cloud Computing Separates Data Center Operations from System Development

Still, Yuri Aguiar knows that the conversation can easily gravitate back to nuts-and-bolts technology if left unchecked. "When you walk out of a technology war room or whiteboard session, you find yourself with a lot of lightning bolts and lines and clouds and boxes, but you never get the stick figures that define the people actually using the stuff. In the old days, we'd have a problem with latency or slow infrastructure. Today, the computing power and the networking services are becoming more and more like dial tone. Now we need to focus on what business users need to get out of the technology. That's just as much an opportunity as it is a challenge. Concentrating IT staff and resources to delivering applications that facilitate the business is the rich epicenter where technology can make a difference in competitive marketplaces."

For Yuri, the combination of services that can be knitted together by IT architects, along with the ability to offload data center worries, is powerful. This arrangement allows architects to spend appropriate time resolving, enabling, or problem-solving issues–all of which couldn't be as easily handled in the past when the same team was burdened with worrying about the data center. To Yuri, "you can't get to the core issues to help the business if you have other distractions."

Paul Saffo explains it this way:

> The IT function is such an all-consuming function that it leaves little time to focus on the strategic. In reality, IT is being asked to handle two very incompatible functions: manage the inner workings of the technology, but also strategically create solutions. It's reminiscent of the saying, "If you like mushroom hunting, then don't become a birdwatcher." You can't look ahead if you also need to look down at the phenomenal minutiae.[5]

Nonetheless, Yuri knows what he's up against in finding the right people to work on creating and delivering business applications at Ogilvy. And he knows his present and future workforce isn't just the younger generation. "We look at the newer IT workforce two ways. It's not just a matter of looking at young workers, but also young-*minded* workers. Age is no barrier to the adoption of technology. Imagine my surprise when my 70-year old mother emailed me not long ago and said, 'Here's my Skype handle.'"

Since Ogilvy happens to study market segments for its clients, Yuri is quick to point out how the "Echo-Boomers" generation (the one right after Generation Y) is the most significant demographic entering the workforce. Before they even enter the workforce, they have already become key drivers of new technology adoption. He's quick to point out that the Nintendo Wii that this generation is growing up on has more computing power than what was on his desk just five years ago. And unlike the generations that preceded them, the Echo-Boomers are not only trained and comfortable with collaborative technologies, they prefer to work and communicate this way.

Do We Need Enterprise Technology Architects or Business Architects?

Yuri has always believed that the applications space needs the best and the brightest. As one of the simplest examples, he points out how some shortsighted companies have built applications that weren't scaled well for the future. Everyone likes the application that was built, but since it can't adapt to growth of the business, the company winds up with a huge problem. It's like a snowball gaining size as it goes downhill, and there's no way to stop it. Those companies learned the hard way that they needed some very bright people with the skills to architect the application correctly in the first place.

Nicholas Carr thinks that in the foreseeable future, there's a big role for architects. Despite the trends he advocates, he feels the role of the architect isn't diminished since it's still up to an individual company (regardless of their cloud decisions) to determine their information architecture. In fact, the architecture can actually be more complex because of all of the potential options and flexibility. "So I think that, particularly in the short term, the architect role will remain, and may even become more important. In smaller companies, it may become more tightly integrated into the business. In the bigger organizations, there may be a central role for an architect to work with other architects embedded within the business lines."

Companies Are Investing in New Business Process Design

How many times have we heard the timeless business school advice of "stick to the knitting"? The point made in countless case studies is that companies that focus on improving and differentiating their core business will win, and those that find themselves weighed down by ancillary distractions will lose. More specifically, owning and maintaining vast data centers is a distraction from the core business of IT end-user companies. If the core competency is running restaurants, or managing hotels, then owning a data center is a distraction—and a costly one at that.

Imagine, then, the company that has completely removed its data center burden from internal operations. Rather than owning and maintaining a data center, they buy it as a service for a monthly fee. Gone are the worries about data center operations and upgrades and service levels. Gone are the capital expenditures and staffing costs and head count. Gone is everything that could be easily bought from an IT service provider, except one thing: the need to apply IT to meet business objectives.

The CIO unburdened by data center worries can now employ a smaller, leaner, more agile team. They won't be worried about traditional IT, and will instead focus on creating business processes that sell more hotel rooms or fill more restaurant seats. Instead of worrying about the processing power to manage an IT application, the CIO's team will focus purely on creating better ways of doing business; of improving the company's core competencies.

This should come as welcome news to line-of-business management. For decades, they've bemoaned the priority gap between traditional IT and the needs of the business. Now the CIO will be able to focus more purely on employing business-savvy architects who can apply IT to changing business processes. In fact, these individuals who work for the CIO won't be known for their traditional IT skills, and will instead be known for their ability to architect solutions. That's why they'll be called business architects.

Futurist Paul Saffo[6] sees opportunity for CIOs who manage this type of business-oriented IT organization. Much like the CFOs of the 1980s and 1990s who went on to become CEOs, he predicts the next generation of CEOs will be coming from today's CIOs. In fact, we're already seeing this. Drugstore.com CEO Dawn Lepore was once CIO at Charles Schwab.

The Critical Importance of Agility

The most powerful player in the twenty-first-century global IT supply chain is the business end user. Since the user has so many options when it comes to consuming IT (ranging from using SaaS packages to developing systems entirely in-house), all the other players in the chain—in-house IT organizations, IT vendors, resellers, and consultants—need to align themselves to respond to end-user needs.

Meanwhile, thanks to the global economy and high-bandwidth Internet connectivity, IT activities that produce value mostly from low-cost and highly efficient operations are being completed where the costs are lowest—outside of the corporate organization. Only those activities delivering value derived through the innovation of highly responsive operations are being completed close to the end user.

Given these broad outlines of the global IT supply chain, the players who need to respond to end-user needs must not only face the concept of agility, but they need to embrace it. In simple terms, agility is the continuous close coordination between business and IT people to respond effectively to constantly changing situations. While some products and services don't require high amounts of agility, others do. Moreover, not everyone is cut out to be agile.

Agility is needed if customers value a product or service primarily because it quickly responds to their evolving needs. If it is valued mostly for its low cost or because of the part it plays in keeping operations running reliably, agility isn't a big factor. What's important in those cases is efficiently maintaining the status quo. The more commoditized a product or service is, the less agility is needed to support it.

Agility Drives Development of New Products and Services

The ultimate in IT agility, however, is epitomized by businesses and services like Google, iTunes, and Facebook, all of which combine an array of technologies to quickly create and deliver new services to a fast-growing and fickle customer base. Their agility keeps them fresh so that their service offerings keep evolving as the needs and tastes of their customers change. If they couldn't keep up with those needs and tastes, their customers would go elsewhere. Somewhere between these two extremes—commodity on one end and agile IT on the other—is where you find most CIOs and their IT organizations.

For reasons of simple economics, businesses will continue to outsource data center and related operations. The efficiencies and economies of scale offered by IT utility companies are already compelling and will only become more so. These IT utilities are evolving from the combination of telecom providers, hardware and software vendors, and data center operators.

As companies outsource the activities that are being handled by IT utilities, they are increasingly turning their attention to the need to be responsive to their customers. That requires agile IT, since everything a company does these days has IT running right down the middle of it. Every new business venture, product, or marketing campaign needs agile IT support to prevent the business end users from being overwhelmed by the flood of details and demands that go along with doing new things. So if they're going to survive, in-house IT groups and the vendors and consultants they work with are going to have to focus primarily on agility and delivering the responsiveness that their business users value.

A Renewed Focus on Using Technology for Profit and Competitive Advantage

Consider the response you would make to the unexpected news that sales of your company's new product X were increasing much faster than had been anticipated, and that customers who bought product X were two-thirds more likely to then purchase product Y in the following 60 days. The way you respond to this unexpected news, and the speed in which you deliver needed systems support, will be the determining factor in how much success you can exploit from the situation.

In this scenario, you need to consider the IT systems that support product X and determine how to scale them up faster than originally planned to handle the extra sales volume. You need to see what new IT support will enable the company to best exploit the emerging opportunity for sales of product Y and figure out how soon that support needs to be in place.

You might decide to launch two projects simultaneously. One project would accelerate the build-out of processing capacity for the systems that support product X. This is the project that is part of improving existing processes and systems; it will deliver more efficiency.

The other project would develop new systems to address the emerging opportunity for product Y and other follow-on product sales. This will create a new process to deal with a new event; it will deliver effectiveness.

How Some Companies Are Driving Agility and Innovation

Business executives can also use agility to boost innovation. An innovative process calls for people to feel a sense of urgency in order to overcome the inertia of doing things the same old way. So placing limits on the time and money that your employees can spend to solve a problem is a great way to create urgency. We are not talking about doing things on the cheap. We are talking about doing them faster and smarter. Challenge yourself and your staff to innovate solutions that cost 10 times less than what your competition is spending and that can be developed four times faster—call it "10/4 performance."

Agility and innovation starts with a frame of mind, and that frame of mind is embodied in a simple three-step process called "Define-Design-Build." It's a simple, easily understood process that guides people through the three steps of developing any new system or business process.

Each step produces a well-defined set of deliverables and tight time boxes that are guidelines for how much time to allocate to each step. See Figure 7.1 for a list of the deliverables and time boxes. Most important is the way that this process enables agility and innovation. Note that this process can be cycled through in 30- to 90-day cycles depending on the size of the development project, the urgency of the project, and other considerations.

In the time boxes beneath each of the three steps there are two sets of recommended times. In larger type is a range of a few weeks or months to spend on each step. These suggested times will move your project along at a good pace. Once people in your company have proved themselves, it may be even more advantageous to adopt an even tighter set of time boxes, and these are shown in smaller type and shown as a small number of days for each step.

The key here is to remember that regardless of the times you choose, this is an iterative approach that does not try to solve all problems at once. Instead, you focus on developing solutions to the most pressing problems first and get those solutions into operation.

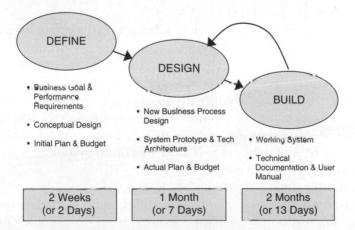

Figure 7.1 Agility and Innovation in a Three-Step Process

Then you iterate again and add additional features as needed. Then keep iterating and adding more features as needed.

Agility Means Move It or Lose

The Define step takes 2 weeks (or can be accelerated to 2 days) and typically costs 5 to 10 percent of the total project budget. The Design step takes 1 month (or accelerated to 7 days) and costs 15 to 30 percent of the total budget. And the Build phase takes 2 months (or accelerated to 13 days) and costs 60 to 80 percent of the total budget.

You may ask, "How do we know these time frames without knowing the specifics of a given project?" Simply put, there is only that much time available if you are truly going to be agile. If people can't define what is needed within two to six weeks, then it certainly won't be an agile project. Likewise, we know the design work will only cost 15 to 30 percent of the total project budget because, if people are spending more than that, they are designing something too complex. More expensive projects will take longer than one to three months to design and then will take too long to build. In sum, if the work cannot meet these requirements, then stop the project because whatever is being done is neither innovative nor agile.

Every project needs a full-time person in charge who has the skills and authority to get things done and is totally committed to success. We call that person the system builder. Without that person, no project can succeed. Make sure you have good system builders for every project you start.

Next, build robust 80 percent solutions rather than attempting to build 100 percent solutions. Avoid the temptation to over-engineer your systems in an attempt to handle every possible combination of events. Trying to build systems that can handle everything increases the cost and complexity in an exponential fashion. Have people, not computers, handle the exceptions and the one-off occurrences, and develop systems to handle only the routine, day-in, day-out transactions. This is how you build systems for 10 times less than your competition.

Remember that big systems are always composed of a collection of smaller subsystems. So once the Define step is completed, big, multimillion-dollar projects can be broken up into smaller projects to develop each subsystem. Instead of one big project team designing everything and then building everything, this arrangement allows multiple smaller teams to design and build subsystems in parallel, under the overall direction of the system builder. This is how to get things done four times faster than your competition.

At first, people may accuse executives who adopt a process such as Define-Design-Build of being overly demanding and unreasonable. But don't relent. What you ask is possible. Development groups can achieve 10/4 performance levels. Give people the training they need and opportunities to learn by doing, but don't lower your standards or extend the time frames.

Notes

1. Nicholas Carr, *The Big Switch: Rewiring the World, from Edison to Google* (New York: W.W. Norton & Company, Inc., 2008).
2. Nicholas Carr, phone interview with authors, February, 2009.
3. Rick Pittard, Chicago, phone interview with authors, February, 2009.
4. Yuri Aguiar, phone interview with authors, February, 2009.
5. Paul Saffo, phone interview with authors, February, 2009.
6. Ibid.

Five Profit Enablers Driving Business to the Cloud

Countless companies and organizations have moved or are moving their more traditional computing environments into the cloud. In fact, according to Ken Male, founder of the New York City–based researcher TheInfoPro, an increasing number of Fortune 2000 companies are investigating cloud computing options. According to Ken, just 20 percent of these organizations he regularly surveys reported they were investigating cloud computing options in early 2009, and that number increased to 42 percent by late 2009.[1] What are the reasons and motivations behind companies moving to the cloud? Are there some key, underlying themes these moves have in common? Just what's driving cloud computing adoption? To see what's really happening, let's take a look at a few examples.

Harvard Medical School

Established by Peter Tonellato in 2008, the Laboratory for Personalized Medicine (LPM) is located in the Center for Biomedical Informatics (CBMI) at Harvard Medical School. In 2009, Dr. Tonellato extended the lab to the Department of Pathology at Beth Israel Deaconess Medical Center, and in 2010 another site was opened in the School of Public Health at the University of Wisconsin in Milwaukee. Currently, laboratory computational work is conducted at all three sites, where individuals collaborate across projects and share the management and use of cloud resources.

The goal of the LPM is to study the confounding questions that arise when personalized medicine is implemented across a hospital's entire care practice to support preventative health care for individuals based on their specific medical, family, and genetic makeup. To do this, the LPM stores, processes, and analyzes human genomes, the vast entirety of an individual's specific hereditary information encoded in approximately 3.2 billion base pairs of that individual's DNA. The raw data for one individual's genome consumes about one-half of a terabyte of data. (A terabyte is equivalent to 1 trillion bytes, which approximates the amount of data contained in literally millions of periodicals and books.)

According to Tonellato, there are currently 12 known individual genome datasets in the world and the LPM actively and routinely analyzes the genomes. Some of the 12 genomes are from well-known individuals like Desmond Tutu, James Watson, and Craig Venter, while others are from anonymous individuals including African tribesmen.

Researchers at the LPM access this vast amount of genome data to conduct ongoing sequencing analysis designed to predict the potential results of medical treatment. For example, the data infrastructure at the LPM allows researchers to create fictitious populations of clinical avatars resulting in millions of hypothetical patient records. This enables the LPM to conduct simulations that estimate not only the health of that hypothetical population, but any health disparities in it. All of this allows limitless research scenarios ranging from preventive health cost analyses, to testing algorithms that can quantify specific risks like breast cancer in women, to identifying the dosing of various types of drugs that are dependent upon an individual's genetic background, to conducting simulations that predict the effectiveness of a particular medical test. While all of this broad research is based on a fictitious population, it paves the way for much smaller and real-life validation studies to be focused and effective when eventually conducted among real people.

When Tonellato started the LPM, he made a conscious decision to house LPM data and research in a cloud computing environment. Based on the options he had, and similar to decisions made for start-up companies, he found the cloud much more attractive than on-premise computer center options as it removed significant worries and reduced ongoing time invested in maintaining IT infrastructure.

"There was significant opportunity cost to consider. If I were to buy 100 servers and turn them over to a central computing organization where the LPM would be at the mercy of the administrators to operate the hardware in a way most conducive to LPM research. The opportunity cost is enormous given the weeks and weeks of lab research staff time required to address hardware, software, and related collaborative administrative operations. Now, after only a year of coordinated LPM research computations on the cloud, the environment and resources are up and running and can be reconfigured and aligned with new projects in a matter of minutes."

Tonellato looked at several offerings and, based on several fundamental issues such as ease of access, breadth of functionality, and costs, settled on the cloud computing environment provided by Amazon Web Services. Tonellato had built data centers before, so he knew about the time and processes that would otherwise be invested in building out a dedicated server farm. To test his theory that the cloud was a desirable alternative, he and his team assessed the flexibility and ease to create custom Amazon Machine Images (AMIs) to support a sophisticated web application and database development environment. His team incorporated private Linux AMIs available from Oracle and quickly deemed the cloud a suitable development platform. Pleased that the solution avoided an entire layer of onsite technology worries, the lab's first web-based application was launched just two weeks later.

The new cloud environment enabled the LPM to manage projects three different ways:

1. Elastic, where the computational exercise of the research is 99 percent of the project and takes advantage of a wide server base

2. Managed elastic, where the researcher might need to compute clusters of 5 or 10 nodes for a relatively limited exercise or might require several replicated 2 to 4-node clusters but are launching and shutting down the cluster(s) from time to time

3. Inelastic, where some projects require a baseline of virtual engines made available all the time to accommodate developers that require constant and consistent online access

To further educate faculty and students about the utility of cloud computing for biomedical research, Tonellato launched a "Clouded"

Translational Science seminar at Harvard Medical School. This seminar fostered collaboration on the cloud between sites at Harvard, area hospital research centers, the University of Wisconsin-Milwaukee, and universities in Japan. Teams of interdisciplinary researchers contributed to DNA and RNA sequencing projects and pilot projects deploying bioinformatic tools and research projects onto the cloud. This exercise led to a set of "best practice" administration and cloud management procedures.

Today, the LPM conducts all research in the cloud. Having built data centers in the past—and now seeing a cloud computing environment delivering what he needs when he needs it—gives Tonellato unique perspective on the reliability and security of the cloud versus traditional, on-premise options. Tonellato feels that IT administrative concerns about cloud security and robustness may be more to avoid early adopter status and perceived risk rather than based on practical substantive risks. According to Tonellato, "Amazon's a lot more worried about my instances staying up and available than I, my lab, Harvard IT administrators, and probably 99 percent of most companies." While he admits that his research environment is inherently different than other sensitive corporate data situations that might be housed in company-maintained data centers, he also feels that the naysayers about cloud security are using perceived risk as opposed to rational risk analysis. "There is nothing simple about risk and security. However well designed, implemented, and managed, security, privacy, and risk reduction practices on public cloud systems have not been demonstrated to be of any less quality than those implemented in similar ways on private environments."

In any case, the value of cloud computing demands that we pursue sound public cloud computing infrastructure development and use.

Golden Gate University

From 2001 to 2008, Anthony Hill was CIO of Golden Gate University (GGU) in San Francisco. During those years, Anthony led a significant transformation of information technology (IT) capabilities in the university and for its students and faculty. GGU was an early adopter of cloud computing and software-as-a-service (SaaS) technologies and has proven this new model of computing to be viable through the full life cycle.

In 2001, Golden Gate University, facing new competition in the face of revenue and profitability pressures, brought in a new senior management team to perform a turnaround to reposition the university in a new competitive marketplace for adult professional education. This new management team led significant change across academics, operations, technology, and financial capitalization.

The turnaround plan called for a renewed focus on technology and a goal of ubiquitous, 24/7 access to all information, transactions, and learning via a Web browser. GGU was behind the technology curve with aging legacy systems, no IT architecture, static web sites, and poor integration. The turnaround plan created pressures to deliver a new business strategy, create a new customer experience, and reduce costs of delivery throughout the enterprise. Essentially, the university articulated an e-business transformation, which required a complete overhaul of its information technology capabilities. A key constraint was that operating costs could not increase. In other words, GGU needed to transform its information technology capabilities, but could not make it more expensive to run IT. IT had to stay cost neutral or, at best, contribute to the bottom line by reducing its costs over time.

The challenge to transform IT capabilities while remaining cost neutral meant that IT had to radically increase its capabilities and output with the same number of people. At that time, the CIO calculated that 90 percent of the IT spend was going into maintenance of existing infrastructure and supporting daily operations. The business technology challenge was to create an IT investment program that created significant new IT value and output, while simultaneously offsetting costs and reallocating staff to activities that provided greater business value.

GGU's CIO created a plan for the university's enterprise IT architecture that heavily leveraged cloud computing. In 2002, an enterprise architecture plan that maximized reliance on early cloud computing and SaaS technologies was a very forward-thinking and an early-adoption of these technologies and this IT management approach. Early in the decade, GGU realized that cloud computing was the most effective approach to realize its goals of a complete IT transformation while also managing to the lowest cost.

The CIO implemented an IT governance process that created clear architectural standards for new IT investments. A fundamental requirement of the new architecture was that all application services must be delivered via a Web browser, and that the applications would be supported as SaaS or hosted solutions.

Two overarching business drivers were at the center of this new IT strategy. First, the business plan required that all business processes and transactions be delivered over the web, enabling the university to effectively function as an e-business. New student and faculty self-service capabilities took cost out of business operations and improved the customer experience. Second, this IT strategy facilitated the reallocation of IT staff from IT operations and maintenance to working on the creation of new IT capabilities that added new value to the university. This was a significant accomplishment as it allowed the same number of people to deliver more new projects focused on new, innovative capabilities to create the future-state architecture required to achieve the goals of the business plan.

From 2002 to 2008, GGU systematically replaced almost every business and learning application from on-premise solutions with web-enabled SaaS solutions. The application portfolio that moved into the cloud included e-learning, ERP (enterprise resource planning) systems, data warehouses, CRM (customer relationship management), fundraising and alumni management, student and faculty email, and collaboration including wikis, blogs, and web conferencing. All these applications were consumed by the university as SaaS applications, and IT staff were no longer required to build and maintain the data center infrastructure required to support them.

Cloud computing and SaaS were two vital levers that lifted the information technology transformation to success. The reallocation of IT costs and labor away from infrastructure management to projects creating new IT capabilities, combined with the delivery of all applications to the staff, faculty, or students, web browser, transformed the organization and the customer experience.

Eventually, the CIO was able to reduce IT staffing budgets by 25 percent as salaries that were focused on maintaining IT infrastructure and applications were no longer needed. Staffing-level reductions were made through natural turnover, and this financial contribution by IT was instrumental in helping restore the university to profitability.

Business benefits included an expansion of the university's market from one that was regional and geographically bound to national and global markets. By 2008 GGU had students on most major continents of the globe. Twenty-four/seven availability of services improved as the applications were delivered from world-class data centers with 24/7 staffing. Significant IT cost reductions were achieved, and IT staff were able to advance their careers building new systems rather than maintaining old ones.

As an early adopter, GGU learned many lessons. It is critical to adhere to the architectural commitment of SaaS applications and leveraging the cloud. The replacement of a single enterprise application is insufficient to reap business benefits of this magnitude. It is only after the enterprise reaches a critical mass of application migration into the cloud that payback on this level can be achieved.

Despite moving applications to the cloud, this case is evidence that an organization still needs to maintain full responsibility for using those applications securely and effectively. The organization is still responsible for the quality of its own data and managing user access to that data. In that respect, the IT function moves to new levels of responsibility in leading these processes and providing integration, information management, and vendor management services.

All of this said, GGU achieved significant levels of payback on its cloud-based investments. From transforming the customer experience to taking cost out of business and IT operations and improving information security, the IT and business strategy of leveraging cloud computing and software-as-a-service technologies continue to pay off for the university.

Silicon Valley Education Foundation

Silicon Valley Education Foundation (SVEF) is the leading foundation focused on ensuring that all students are prepared for college and careers. They do this by focusing in the critical areas of STEM (science, technology, engineering, and math). With an increasing gap of qualified workers to take over Silicon Valley jobs, SVEF feels that the Silicon Valley's future as the heart of U.S. innovation is at risk—so their goal is to be the leading advocate for public education in the Silicon Valley. They do this by establishing effective partnerships with the private sector, the education community, and other organizations to support specific areas of need in public education. They focus on achieving results for the students, families, teachers, educators, and business leaders they serve.

SVEF delivers programs by partnering with organizations that support their mission of improving public education. These programs include:

- Investments in improving science, technology, engineering, and math education
- Forums bringing together top business, education, and civic leaders
- Educating families on school readiness
- Leveraging technology to allow teachers to collaborate and share high-quality lesson plans and teaching resources
- Providing monetary grants of $500 to $1,000 for teachers who submit innovative lesson plans
- Partnering with organizations that share the same educational mission, like Silicon Valley Community Foundation, Hispanic Foundation of Silicon Valley, the Tech Museum, the Krause Center for Innovation, and Technet
- Researching policy and exemplary programs while advocating for the resources that support student success

According to SVEF CEO Muhammed Chaudhry, "Success in the classroom is getting kids ready for college." But when it comes to managing their own technology used by SVEF to meet their goals, Chaudhry is very clear. "We don't want to manage a lot of technology. We are in the education business, not the technology business." An example of that philosophy is SVEF's migration to cloud computing to enable deployment of its Lessonopoly.org tool designed for teachers to manage their lesson plans online.

After extensive research, SVEF concluded that it would be valuable to provide a technology-based approach to assisting teachers with their lesson plans that serve as the building blocks of individual class sessions. In the past, lesson plans have been paper-based, with no ability to contain or link to rich data sources that can be used in individual lessons. For example, video can be a rich resource for teaching many subjects, but paper-based lesson plans can, at best, list the online location of a relevant video. Furthermore, paper-based lesson plans are a poor medium for collaboration, making it difficult for experienced teachers to share knowledge and best practices with less experienced colleagues.

Therefore, SVEF developed Lessonopoly, a Web 2.0 application facilitating lesson plan creation, modification, and sharing. Lessonopoly offers the ability to link rich data sources to lesson plans; these data sources may be stored within Lessonopoly itself or on another server located on the Internet. Lessonpoly offers users the ability to rate and comment upon individual lesson plans, thereby offering user-based quality control. In addition, it offers search functionality to allow users to seek lesson plans by title, content, or description. Finally, Lessonopoly allows creation of new lesson plans by editing one or more existing lesson plans and saving the updated document as a new lesson plan. This facilitates teacher customization of material to suit the needs of their classes.

In its original configuration, Lessonopoly was installed on a single server. This poses a risk, since hardware failure could result in system unavailability until repairs were made. If a component like a network card or a motherboard were to fail, a day or more could pass before system availability was restored. If a disk drive were to fail, not only would the device need to be replaced, but also the system would need to be restored from backup, taking even longer. This vulnerability would be worse if system load required additional hardware to enable the application tiers to be spread across multiple servers. Each server poses hardware failure risk at its level, which impacts total application availability; in essence, moving to a multitier hardware topology raises overall system risk.

Because reducing Lessonopoly risk via virtualization and additional hardware would cost more than SVEF wanted to spend, HyperStratus, a cloud computing advisory, and SVEF agreed to evaluate whether a cloud implementation would be appropriate for Lessonopoly. Amazon Web Services (AWS) was selected as the target cloud implementation to evaluate. Because AWS, as part of its internal architecture, uses virtualization, SVEF would be shielded from the risk of hardware failure. In addition, should individual instances of the SVEF application crash, restart is easy and therefore downtime is kept to a minimum.

Amazon describes AWS as "an infrastructure web services platform in the cloud. With AWS you can requisition compute power, storage, and other services—gaining access to a suite of elastic IT infrastructure services as your business demands them." AWS can be characterized as "infrastructure-as-a-service." This means that

Amazon provides basic computing capability—a virtual machine container, reliable and redundant storage, and high-performance networking—in a remote location. Users have no need to provision or pay for local hardware infrastructure—Amazon takes care of that. Users focus on the software assets—the applications—that reside upon and use AWS computing resources.

AWS is comprised of a number of individual services; the key services for the needs of Lessonopoly are these four:

1. Elastic Compute Cloud (EC2)
2. Simple Storage Services (S3)
3. Elastic IP Addresses
4. Elastic Block Storage

Prior to using the cloud, the environment for Lessonopoly depended on dedicated hardware equipped with the Fedora Core Linux operating system. In time, this would prove to lack the robustness and scalability needed for daily backup and room for growth. SVEF realized that it would eventually need to add more servers and hard drives, and would need to invest a significant amount of time to provision them.

With the help of HyperStratus, SVEF considered a proposal to move the environment into the cloud as an alternative to an investment in more hardware. If it were to take this approach, it would convert the process of ordering hardware, waiting for it to arrive and then provisioning it to a much simpler step of creating the cloud environment with just several clicks. At what would be a reasonable cost, Lessonopoly could be up and running with more than enough available servers in just a few minutes rather than days. HyperStratus also provided a cost analysis comparing the cloud solution to a more traditional hosting environment, which enabled a decision to go with the efficiency and scalability that the AWS solution provides.

After making the decision to move Lessonopoly to the cloud, SVEF found that migration and acclimation to the new environment was straightforward. It only took one day to migrate three servers to the cloud and to have Lessonopoly up and running. Ultimately, the move from three physical servers to the cloud resulted in a monthly cost of just one-fourth to one-third of the previous hosting solution.

Beachbody.com

Beachbody, the creator of the nation's most popular in-home fitness and weight loss solutions, was founded in 1998 by Product Partners, LLC, of Los Angeles. Offering innovative, results-oriented programs and skilled, motivational trainers, Beachbody's core purpose is to help people achieve their fitness goals and enjoy a healthy, fulfilling life. Beachbody's many programs—including P90X, Slim in 6, INSANITY, Turbo Jam, Hip Hop Abs, Yoga Booty Ballet, Kathy Smith's Project: YOU! Type 2, and ChaLEAN Extreme—combine challenging DVD-based home fitness programs with diet guidelines, nutritional supplements, and an online support system.

To do this, Beachbody.com provides 24/7 motivational and peer support through message boards, led by Beachbody customers who have enjoyed success with the products. Customer nurturing is key to Beachbody's marketing and business growth. In fact, Beachbody.com has approximately 45,000 visitors per day and approximately 100,000 page views daily. The message boards include approximately 1.26 million members, with an average of 95,000 page views per day. Add to that how Beachbody's products have become increasingly popular—fueled by consumer interest in avoiding health club memberships in favor of getting fit at home with inexpensive DVDs—and the result is a huge window of opportunity.

For Steve Winshel, CIO of Beachbody.com, the trajectory from $100 million in company revenue to $350 million in just a few short years has challenged his technology strategy to prepare for continued growth. It's also allowed him to consider cloud solutions to shoulder the expansion. According to Winshel, ''I'm happy to have someone else deal with the range of issues like servers and fault tolerance and failover and PCI compliance–as long as I know they are dealing with it properly.''

All of this said, the speed demanded by the business has created unique pressures on the e-commerce strategy. As is the case in many fast-growing online retail businesses, job one of the e-commerce system is to be highly available, consistent, PCI compliant, capable of good reporting and—above all—rock solid in capturing orders. But Beachbody requires a second, more complex and strategic requirement of its e-commerce platform: extreme flexibility.

To fuel growth, Beachbody must constantly test offers, adjusting telemarketing scripts as many as five times a day. (Some businesses may test just five times a week.) Moreover, the results of those tests can impact offers in their television advertising. The need for this extreme flexibility is baked into the culture of the company: it just moves fast. "When it comes to the web, we need to know traffic is being split properly for offer tests using an a/b split. We need to be as nimble online as we are with our telemarketing," Winshel says. "We need flexibility in making changes to the system, in running tests. Not just pricing changes, but testing different upsell flow and feature sets. This means we need to be able to make significant changes to content and look and feel in the e-commerce system. And many vendors don't have a tool that is as flexible as we need."

To meet the need, Winshel created a unique agreement with his e-commerce provider. It takes advantage of Winshel's desire to let a reliable vendor manage a mission-critical e-commerce environment, but also allows for his internal team to share development. This gives his team unique flexibility in crafting and testing new offers in real time while relieving the burden of managing e-commerce in house.

Five Profit Enablers Driving Business to the Cloud . . . and Away from Corporate Data Centers

It's long been said that water seeks its own level. In free markets, companies will similarly migrate to more competitive solutions that enable their profit objectives. On a microeconomic and macroeconomic scale over a period of decades, organizations will establish a changing equilibrium in the market based on the newest methods to legally and reliably produce profits. Cloud computing is changing the equilibrium underneath the foundations of today's corporate data centers.

After evaluating case studies in this chapter along with others, we've identified the following five most dominant themes that are driving organizations to move their business into the cloud:

1. *Cloud computing enables clearer focus on the business.* In their popular management book *In Search of Excellence*,[2] Tom Peters and Robert Waterman popularized the well-established theory that companies with an unwavering focus on their core business are more likely to succeed. Their ability to "stick to the knitting" by maintaining an unobstructed focus

on what matters most—their core competence, honing their business expertise, customers, and mission—gave them a distinct advantage over their competitors.

Business professionals who are weaving cloud computing into their business processes frequently comment on how they are in the education, manufacturing, or financial services or any number of businesses—but that they "don't want to be in the technology business." They understand that, unlike in the pre-Internet era, technology is now indigenous to their products and services—that it is woven into their marketing, product delivery, and internal business processes. It's part of the fabric of business just like capital, communications, selling, hiring, electricity, lights, and plumbing. From that point of view, they want to divest their worry about the mechanics of technology—data centers, networks, storage, e-commerce, and the like—in order to concentrate precious financial and human resources on how to generate more profits and better business outcomes in their category. They view the alternative as the need to spend significant attention on maintaining and funding computing capacity—and an unwanted distraction that dilutes the efficiency of the organization and its focus on core business objectives.

Simply put, cloud computing is attractive to more and more businesses because it allows them to focus on what matters most—their customers, their business processes, and the employees who nurture them.

2. *Cloud computing reduces dependence on internal infrastructure and the capital expense that goes with that infrastructure.* In our discussions with business executives and IT professionals moving their environments to the cloud, many describe a decision-making process something like this: "Why should I buy 100 servers for my applications when I'll not only need to onboard them, provision them, and then turn them over to my corporate data center staff—and I'll then be dependent upon their staff and cost to maintain them? I am at their mercy—and their available time—as they service the rest of our corporate landscape."

In larger business environments, it's this very worry that's driving increasing pockets of applications inside the business to seek cloud alternatives. New economic realities combined with new business initiatives are empowering lines within large corporations to self-fund their own computing that, in many cases, is more cost-effective as an operating expense than if capitalized by incremental, company-owned infrastructure.

Similarly, smaller enterprises and start-ups are moving directly to the cloud as they expand or create ground-up applications. They are motivated to choose the cloud primarily by the lack of either sufficient or any available infrastructure. More often than not, a small organization's limited budgets make cloud alternatives attractive right out of the gate. Cloud decision making in smaller enterprises is often less about whether to consider internal infrastructure and more about seeking the best paths in the cloud.

In all cases where companies have moved to the cloud, we've found that the business leaders responsible are happy to shed the worry about maintaining more corporate infrastructure as long as they are reasonably guaranteed the reliability and security their applications require.

3. *Cloud computing automatically scales up and down with business volume, and this variable cost operating model reduces financial risks.* As we talk to people driving cloud initiatives, we learn more about how important scalability and agility have become. Unlike more fixed infrastructure in traditional corporate data centers or development environments, cloud resources expand and contract depending upon the amount of use, traffic, and bandwidth required. This has become a critical enabler of business efficiency as technology is sewn more pervasively into business processes and customer experiences.

Competitors in today's business world emerge quickly and without warning. Unlike the days when large corporate brands took years to build their brands, newer companies like Yahoo!, Google, Twitter, and Facebook prove how the Internet has accelerated product adoption to lightning speed. This has created an environment where companies need to move swiftly—in minutes, hours, and days rather than weeks and months—to bring their products and services to market and continually adjust them as market feedback indicates.

Employing agility in business today is imperative, and the cloud delivers the flexibility that is called for. In our conversations with those tapping the cloud, they consistently talk about how quickly and easily cloud providers deliver elasticity based on customer and user demands. This on-demand flexibility removes the worry associated with whether or not internal data center infrastructure will present constraints and service interruptions during peak periods.

Much like we expect electricity and water in our homes to be available worry free in the quantities we need at any given time, cloud computing providers can—if well chosen and directed—deliver computing resources on demand.

4. *In-house systems can be migrated to the cloud with relative ease if the process is well designed.* Although cloud computing environments vary significantly—whether they involve software-as-a-service, platform-as-a-service, infrastructure-as-a-service, or varied combinations of the three—the migration required of in-house systems can be relatively simple. There are three primary drivers easing the migration process.

First, providers are inherently motivated to make the process as simple as possible for the customer—both by contract and because contract perpetuation is the lifeblood of their revenue. In order to do business in a highly competitive environment where options are increasing (and continue to include solutions managed in-house), providers are acutely aware that they must make migration as simple as possible for their new customers in order to compete.

Second, as customers investigate cloud options, their RFP (request for proposal) process and careful construction of SLAs (service-level agreements) result in agreements that typically plan for successful migration. Granted, this requires a certain amount of smart planning before contract signature; however, this up-front work yields efficiencies upon execution of the contract deliverables.

Third, while some cloud environments can be complex and require much more sophisticated migration planning and execution than others, there are just as many implementations that involve straightforward, ground-up launches or transfers of existing environments to a cloud provider's infrastructure. Naturally, as the industry has continued to acclimate to and gather experience with more implementations, the migration process has and will continue to streamline.

5. *Cloud computing is competitively priced, allowing customers to buy only what they consume.* Without question, one of the most significant threats cloud computing presents to traditional corporate data center environments is the pricing model. Cloud providers can compete because their capacity, security, and expertise—which is often much larger than an in-house option—can be sold on a pay-as-you-need basis. Nowhere is the analogy to public utilities more meaningful than with pricing. Just as the common household wouldn't capitalize and fuel a fixed-cost generator and leave it running 100 percent of the time to provide energy to their home, the cloud offers computing consumption models and pricing that invoices based on resources used—just like public water and electric utilities.

In case study after case study, this translates into real savings for customers. The capital cost to purchase 100 servers and the additional ongoing operational expenses needed to support them can be fairly straightforward to calculate. Cloud providers know this and price their services competitively not only because they can, but because they know that lower cost provides substantial justification to move applications and infrastructure into the cloud.

Notes

1. Ken Male, TheInfoPro Servers Research Wave 7 (Spring 2009) and Wave 8 (Fall 2009).
2. Tom Peters and Robert Waterman, *In Search of Excellence: Lessons from America's Best-Run Companies* (New York: Grand Central Publishing, 1988) [orig. pub. 1982].

CHAPTER
9

The Business Impact of Cloud Computing

In order to cope with unpredictability, companies need to reduce their fixed costs. What were once considered, in a more predictable economy, normal amounts of fixed cost as a percentage of total revenue are no longer a general rule. To survive, companies need to focus on achieving low break-even points for their operations. If a company can break even at utilization rates of 50 percent or less, it then has room to maneuver to meet the sudden and unexpected fluctuations in product demand and market prices in today's less predictable economy. The more a company can turn fixed costs into variable costs, the more maneuvering room it gains.

Through this economic necessity, more and more companies are shifting away from the constraints of rigid, fixed cost operating models and are trading them for variable cost business models that enable them to respond more quickly to changing market conditions. This approach is better suited to our present economy because it reduces dependence on (and risk related to) large, up-front capital investments to enter new markets or launch new products. This flexible cost structure protects cash flow because operating expenses rise and fall in alignment with revenue.

New Economic Engines for Growth

Just as the industrial technology of the last century enabled the creation of the assembly line that delivered profits from economies of scale, information technology of this century enables the creation of the agile and responsive enterprise that delivers profits from continuous response to changing market conditions and customer needs. The responsive enterprise, by necessity, uses a variable cost operating model because it is too expensive and risky to be responsive using traditional fixed cost models.

In the last century, business models were largely based on a fixed cost operating model driven by large capital investments to leverage economies of scale. Incremental profits were produced by turning out ever increasing volumes of standard products and spreading operating expenses over larger and larger numbers of units sold. This model worked as long as product demand was reasonably predictable and stable because companies could then allocate labor and capital to optimize production and return on investment.

But when product life cycles are shortened to months instead of years and when the predictability of mass markets is replaced with the uncertainty of a global real-time economy and rapidly evolving consumer preferences, the capital-intensive fixed cost business model no longer works. The real-time economy of this century is composed of many smaller and rapidly evolving market segments where customers want more than just low-priced products. Companies must constantly evolve their products to respond to market needs.

A graphic case in point that illustrates this is the evolution of the mobile phone. In the last years of the twentieth century, Motorola made the most reliable mobile phones at the lowest prices. Their efficient manufacturing processes enabled them to dominate mobile phone markets around the world. Yet since the turn of the century, Motorola has seen its low-cost mobile phones become commoditized and marginalized as they lost customers to a succession of new entrants into the market. Each new entrant offered products that cost a little more and were often a little less reliable but that responded to evolving customer needs. First came Nokia, responding to customer needs that a mobile phone be a fashion statement; then came Research in Motion's BlackBerry, responding to business executives' desire to combine phone and email into one small device; and now Apple with its iPhone has created a whole new category by responding to a mix of desires that, among other things, can store many applications on one highly coveted device.

The most responsive and low-risk way to explore new market segments and develop new products is to use business units with variable cost operations supported by cloud-based and software-as-a-service (SaaS) systems. Companies adopting variable cost cloud computing services will see their total IT spend versus company revenue go down even as IT spend versus total company operating expenses actually goes up. This is because, in many contemporary businesses, business operations and IT are so closely intertwined that there is hardly any meaningful distinction left between the two, so variable IT expenses will rise as business grows. But it will also drop as business volumes drop, so it is a low-risk way to protect cash flow while operating in new or unpredictable markets.

Companies moving to this operational model from traditional, fixed cost operating models are creating demand for products and services based on a group of related technologies like cloud computing and server and network virtualization. Cloud and virtualization services are provided to customers on a variable cost, pay-as-you-go basis determined by the number of users and their volume of transactions. Suppliers of cloud computing and virtualization products and services have seen their stock prices perform well. This is an important indicator of the shift companies are making to variable cost operating models.[1]

Time to Get Agile and Reinvent Traditional Business Operations

Irving Wladawsky-Berger believes a major impact of cloud computing on business is the trend to outsourcing support activities and then collaborating closely with an extended network of suppliers and customers. In his words:

> Cloud computing, I believe, represents the evolution of IT towards an Internet-based computing model explicitly designed to enable the transition from inside-out to outside-in organizations.
>
> More and more, a company needs to be focused on the world outside its boundaries, not only because much of its work is now being done with outside partners, but in order to better understand our fast-changing market environment so it can make better business decisions, as well as to better respond to the varying requirements of its clients, so it can provide each of them the best possible products and services.[2]

Dr. Wladawsky-Berger believes cloud computing combined with the wide availability of high-speed Internet connections is ushering in an era where computing power, data, and application systems can be delivered and consumed anywhere on demand. The first wave of cloud computing services has begun to standardize the delivery of infrastructure like computing power, data storage, and software platforms.

The next wave of services will go beyond infrastructure and will standardize and deliver mass customized services for companies and individuals. These will be standard processes for activities like accounting, human resources, and finance. Cloud computing will enable companies to acquire more than just software but whole business services as a real-time outsourced service.

He notes that the use of standardized services in the manufacturing industries has brought major improvements in productivity and quality over the past three decades. So there is most likely an opportunity to use cloud-based business services in companies to bring similar productivity and quality improvements to customer-facing and front-office activities.

Peter Fingar is an author and observer of the evolving relationship between business and IT. His thinking about the impact of cloud computing on business operations is presented in his book, *Dot.Cloud: The 21st Century Business Platform.*[3]

He believes cloud computing will transform how companies access information, how they share content, and how they interact with their customers as well as suppliers. Cloud computing changes the economics of business, allowing companies to adapt and scale their business models to market conditions. He sees cloud computing as a way to harness the Internet to: (1) spread computing tasks across multiple clusters of machines; (2) provide a real-time and interactive platform for developing and delivering new products and services; (3) provide a platform for human collaboration; and (4) make the world's information accessible anywhere.

He believes the last decade was about the World Wide Web of information and the power of connecting content, but the future is more about people connecting and collaborating to get work done. It's about execution on new ideas and new ways of working. Business processes are how work gets done, and the cloud will become the place where those processes reside and are managed.

The cloud makes it possible for multiple companies to come together to work as one value delivery system, not just for efficiency but, more importantly, for responsiveness and innovation. But these new organizational forms can't be managed like the factory of old, for each participating business runs on its own clock using its own internal rules and methods. In the twenty-first century, Industrial Age command-and-control leadership gives way to connect-and-collaborate, where every member of a business team is a leader. In the cloud, leaders don't give commands, they transmit information, trusting the team members' competencies and gaining accountability through transparency. True leadership is about cooperation, not control. Transparency becomes the invisible hand of management control.[4]

Irving Wladawsky-Berger and Peter Fingar point out some interesting developments that fall into two main areas. First is the changing relationship between a company and its suppliers and customers in the new outside-in organization. Second is the change in the leadership paradigm from the Industrial Age command-and-control model to the present connect-and-collaborate model.

Get Ready, Get Set, Go: Success in a Real-Time Economy

A study of 400 companies conducted from 1998 to 2004 by Diamond Management and Technology Consultants reinforces what Dr. Howard Rubin's research found, as reported in Chapter 2 in the section titled "The Patterns Reveal an Interesting Story." And the findings of Dr. Rubin's study map right into the developments pointed out by Wladawsky-Berger and Fingar.

The Diamond Management and Technology Consultants study, titled "Don't Waste a Crisis," found that companies succeeding during those years followed seven practices.[5] These practices can be categorized into three groups. The first group of practices—one, two, and three—relates to how a company structures its operating model to best adapt to high change and unpredictable markets. (This group could be called "Get Ready.") Practices four and five—the second group—are concerned with how a company selects the markets it will serve along with how it communicates with customers and prospects in those markets. (This group could be called

"Get Set.") The third group contains practices six and seven and describes company strategies for success in the markets they have selected. (This group could be called "Go.")

The seven practices revealed in the study are:

1. *Cut the right expenses by getting at root-cause expenses.* Everyone can cut costs, but only some are able to cut the right costs. Successful companies avoid shortsighted chopping of costs and instead find ways to leverage their spending to improve productivity and cut total company operating expenses.

2. *Automate, automate, automate.* Automate operations when they become routine, and avoid trying to automate rapidly evolving operations. It is easier and cheaper to automate routine operations because they are routine and it is much more expensive to automate complicated operations where rules are constantly changing. Find those operations where people are doing the same things over and over again and make the investments needed to automate them. This delivers operating efficiencies.

3. *Use vendors to drive down total cost and "variablize" costs.* Find vendors who have aggregated customer demand for certain operations and made investments to drive down the cost of those operations through economies of scale. These vendors can offer their services at lower rates than a company would pay if it did them in-house. By outsourcing these operations to such vendors, a company can migrate to a variable cost operating model. By paying only for the capacity it needs, a company gets flexibility to ramp up and ramp down their usage and operating expenses to meet changing business conditions.

4. *Identify customers to grow with.* Instead of catering to all customers, companies can focus on key customers where their products are mission critical and build strong relationships with them. Companies find ways to wrap their products with a tailored blanket of value-added services that customize them for their customers and thus make them more valuable. Learn when to let go of traditional customers who are not growing or are shrinking and who want only the lowest prices. It is very hard to make money with these customers.

5. *Optimize their marketing mix.* Focus sales and marketing efforts on market segments and customers who value a company's

products and services the most. Find ways to communicate with these customers in a continuous and real-time manner so as to understand what they want and strengthen relationships with them. Social media like Facebook, Twitter, and YouTube offer ways to do this at minimal cost.

6. *Invest when others did not/invented their future.* Invest in new capabilities to deliver products and services in times when competitors do not. When competitors are hunkered down it's easier to move into new markets. If a company knows where it wants to go and what it needs to do while others are undecided, that is the best time for it to make its moves.

7. *Put all their eggs in one or only a few baskets.* Companies need to concentrate on their strengths and not get distracted. They need to focus new investments in their core areas of expertise or in developing new strengths to respond to evolving conditions in their most important markets as well as attract and keep profitable customers in those markets.

Interconnected, Adaptable, and Specialized

We live in a world where it is clear that companies must keep their cost of doing business low and as variable as possible and at the same time continuously tailor their products to meet changing customer demands. They need to make it simple and convenient for customers to find them, contact them, and do business with them. In addition, companies need to have connections to their customers and suppliers that enable them to collaborate effectively and transact business efficiently.

If we apply the seven practices identified earlier and use them to guide how a company might structure itself, then we get a business model that displays the characteristics of being adaptable, interconnected, and specialized.[6] These characteristics are directly related to the three practice groups. The group called "Get Ready" calls for companies to move to variable costs whenever possible so as to be adaptable to fluctuating markets. The "Get Set" practices call for companies to select specific market segments and customers and create robust connections with those customers. And the "Go" group calls for companies to specialize in their core functions that produce the value-add for its customers. Figure 9.1 illustrates what this business model looks like.

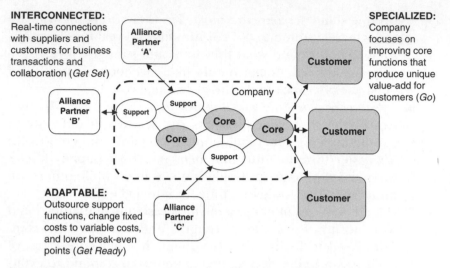

INTERCONNECTED:
Real-time connections with suppliers and customers for business transactions and collaboration (*Get Set*)

SPECIALIZED:
Company focuses on improving core functions that produce unique value-add for customers (*Go*)

ADAPTABLE:
Outsource support functions, change fixed costs to variable costs, and lower break-even points (*Get Ready*)

Figure 9.1   Company and Network of Alliance Partners and Customers

A Simple Taxonomy of Business Systems

We can extend this business model further to provide a simple way to think about the systems that companies need to implement a business operating model like the one illustrated in Figure 9.1. Companies need three categories of systems:

1. Interconnecting systems
2. Adaptive systems
3. Specialization systems

Interconnecting systems use text, voice, and video to link a company with its prospects, its customers, and its suppliers in order to exchange data related to routine business activities, like placing orders and paying invoices, and also to collaborate as needed on common projects. A company must be convenient to do business with; the sales, marketing, and customer service groups of a company need to be easy to contact; and information about its products must be readily available and quickly understandable.

Examples of systems in this category are all types of social media like Facebook, Twitter, YouTube, and so on. Also in this category are application systems, like Google Docs, GoToMeeting, Skype, and WebEx, that enable collaboration among workgroups at different companies and in different geographical locations. This category includes the Internet itself along with various wireless Internet connections and electronic data interchange (EDI) systems.

Adaptive systems enable a company to monitor what is happening in their internal operations and in their interactions with their customers and suppliers. These are systems that allow a company to adjust its daily operations to meet market conditions and control its own costs of doing business. This includes traditional systems like accounting/ERP (enterprise resource planning), purchasing, HR/payroll, financial reporting, and budgeting.

Because variable cost business operations are achieved by outsourcing support activities to supplier partners, it is important for companies to respond quickly as events unfold and problems or opportunities arise. Adaptive systems are not static regulatory systems and instead sense and respond in a timely manner. In doing so, they enable the company to maximize its operating performance.

Two kinds of new adaptive systems address this need: business process management (BPM) along with business intelligence (BI) and analytics. BPM systems enable operations staff to: 1) watch the internal performance of their business units; 2) performance of transactions between their company and their customers and suppliers; and 3) on an hourly and daily basis. BPM systems enable people to take corrective action in real time as needed to keep operations flowing smoothly. BI systems provide staff and management with relevant information to help in decision making and they provide analytics useful for spotting new trends. (These two kinds of systems and their potential are also discussed in Chapter 6.)

Specialization systems enable a company to understand what customers want and continuously evolve existing products to meet changing customer needs. These systems also support the design and roll out new products as opportunities arise and provide the operating support that drives a company's value creation activities. They enable the design and delivery of the products or services that its customers buy.

Examples of application systems in this category could be customer contact and relationship management systems, all manner of graphic design systems and music and video production systems, job scheduling and delivery management systems, and sales support and customer service systems.

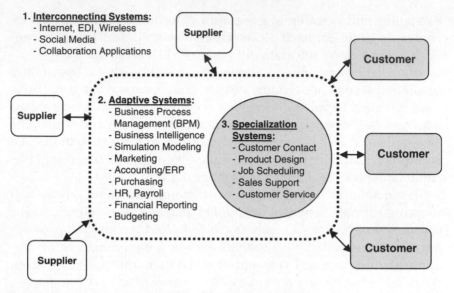

Figure 9.2   Three Categories of Business Systems

These three categories of business systems are illustrated in Figure 9.2.

Cloud-Based Systems for the Three Categories

A company needs an appropriate mix of capabilities and capacity in the three categories of systems shown in Figure 9.2. Depending on the size of a company and its existing installed base of legacy systems, it makes sense to use some mix of cloud-based and in-house systems, however, for start-up companies, it may be logical to use cloud-based systems for all of its needs. Then if the start-up reaches positive cash flow and starts to grow its revenue, it can consider when it might need to move from cloud systems to more traditional in-house or hosted systems.

Interconnecting systems are already delivered largely over the Internet, so cloud-based systems in this category make sense for companies of all sizes. Social media are already cloud-based along with collaboration applications like Google Docs, WebEx, or GoToMeeting, so companies are quickly figuring out how to use them to communicate and collaborate. Cloud options are also available for companies to acquire basic communications, computing infrastructure, data storage, and system management capabilities. These are referred to as infrastructure-as-a-service (IaaS) and platform-as-a-service (PaaS).

SaaS applications exist for most of the adaptive systems that companies need. The question about whether to use SaaS versions of these systems or traditional in-house systems depends on each company's installed base of legacy systems and the software user and support contracts related to these systems. As these contracts come up for renewal, companies should take the opportunity to evaluate the feasibility of switching to SaaS applications.

There are more and more SaaS applications now available that address a range of different business functions from ERP to human resources, from CRP to project management. These systems can be expanded upon and modified with additional features through service-oriented architecture (SOA) and mashups. (These technologies are explained in more detail in Chapter 3.) In this way companies can begin to gain experience in combining their legacy systems with new systems that are cloud and SaaS based.

Collaboration Is Now More Profitable than Control

Companies need to work more closely with networks of suppliers to achieve an effective variable cost business model (the outside-in organization structure described by Wladawsky-Berger). The simplistic but relentless pursuit of money alone can't produce the profits it once did since this money-only focus causes companies to optimize efficient production of existing products, but at the expense of the ability to change and create new products as markets evolve. As discussed in Chapter 1, companies optimized for efficiency are like cars optimized for speed. They go fast and work fine as long as the road is straight; but when the road twists and turns they can't handle the corners and they crash. Winding roads need cars that are highly responsive, not just fast.

There is an inescapable tension between efficiency and responsiveness. They're at opposite ends of a spectrum. Companies have to position themselves at a point on the continuum that best meets the company's present circumstances. As circumstances change, the company needs to keep repositioning itself. Failure to continuously reevaluate and reposition has been the downfall of many, once-reputable, Industrial Age companies in the last decade; they positioned themselves at the efficiency end of the continuum for too long while their markets evolved and customers found other companies to meet their needs.

This tendency to focus too much on efficiency is apparent when a company's senior management is quoted making statements such as, "We'll eliminate cost and increase efficiency in our supply chain and our business operations." This is code-speak used when companies are attempting to implement systems that give them excessive control over their suppliers in the name of achieving greater efficiency.

These systems simply shift profits from smaller suppliers to the bigger, more powerful companies, and then the more powerful companies become complacent with their profits and suppliers lose motivation to do anything new because they aren't making money. Ultimately, when the market changes, everybody (the whole supply chain of companies and suppliers) flies off the road and crashes as demand for existing products suddenly drops and new products haven't been developed.

Wealth is created today by supply chains and other business networks that enable companies to better collaborate and coordinate their activities so they keep up with changing markets and deliver new products that customers want. (This is the connect-and-collaborate organization described by Fingar). When companies discover what customers really want, they naturally find that those same customers want a good price—but that doesn't mean it's got to be the lowest price. People want products that keep responding to their changing needs and circumstances and they are willing to pay a premium for them.

The iPhone or the iPad is a classic example of this type of organizing and operating. It's not made by one company. It is a rapidly changing mix of tangible and intangible values and features delivered via a mix of hardware and software that is responsive to evolving needs of its growing customer base. There are profits to be made by everybody in the iPhone supply chain because customers will pay more for the product—one that has adapted to changing customer needs. The iPhone is a like a symphony orchestra; Apple is the conductor of the orchestra, but it's just one party involved in the process creating its success. Companies in the iPhone orchestra pay attention to Apple and coordinate their actions with each other to keep up with the fast pace of change. They are motivated to play well in the orchestra because they are all making money, or at least believe that they soon will. Apple isn't trying to create all the innovation itself; everybody is innovating and coordinating with each other to keep the ball rolling because iPhone is more than a mobile phone; it's a growing ecosystem of products and services that has now taken on a life of its own.

In stark contrast, single companies using their own factories once designed and made products of the industrial economy. In today's information economy, supply chains of interrelated companies work together to evolve products in constant response to market changes. As more and more products follow a trajectory like the mobile phone, a huge opportunity will unfold to provide collaboration platforms for businesses to create and deliver new, innovative products. Supply chains and other business operations that require cooperation between multiple companies will be reinvented, and traditional business practices will be enhanced by ones enabled by collaboration systems that are hosted on cloud platforms and delivered through SaaS.

Necessity Makes Radical the New Normal

It's 10:30 on a weekday morning. Do you know what people in the operating units of your company are up to? They've been pretty quiet lately, and not making much of a fuss over that backlog of computer system enhancements they used to bring up all the time. Maybe they've finally settled down and accepted that they need to make do with what they've got, especially those ERP and CRM systems your company spent so much time and money installing.

But the quiet might not mean they've simply accepted their situation and deferred their requests. Business situations keep changing, and people's needs are more pressing than ever. All that talk about why people "have to make do with systems they already have" and accept constraints imposed by data security issues and accounting regulations hasn't really changed anybody's mind. In many companies, businesspeople have simply moved on from the subject and are doing what they need to do whether or not they get official permission.

They are still keeping up appearances about using company ERP systems and dutifully run numbers and orders through them, but that's just back-office stuff. The new work, the cutting-edge stuff, is being handled by systems patched together with tools at hand that people can put together themselves: spreadsheets, email, texting, along with cloud computing, SaaS, and mashup applications that they rent on a month-to-month basis for small amounts of money they pay out of their expense accounts and operating budgets.

People are under pressure. They need to keep rolling out new products and services and enhancing old ones. They need to keep finding new ways to engage customers and prospects. People know that money talks, and that they need to keep bringing in new revenue or else their positions will be cut and they'll be let go. They're ignoring IT-business-as-usual excuses for why things can't be done. They aren't waiting for that great new system you say you're going to deliver sometime in the fourth quarter this year, or maybe next year . . . or the year after.

The pressure of economic necessity has brought about a changed mind-set and an approach that might have seemed radical not that many years ago, but nonetheless, that is what is happening. People are doing what they have to do to make progress. When the going gets tough, the tough get agile.

Three Laws of Business Agility

There seem to be three laws that govern the practice of business and IT agility. The first one defines why we need to be agile, the second identifies how to best achieve agility, and the third shows where agility can yield the greatest results.

To begin with, agility is no longer just a good idea. It's now backed by law, the law of probability. This law says if a company can't keep up with rapid rates of change in the world, then its probability of success will get smaller and smaller every day. And since companies need IT infrastructure and applications to operate just as our bodies need nervous systems and muscles to move, IT agility is required if a company is going to achieve business agility.

Effective support of business agility is rapidly becoming the primary reason a company has an internal IT group (versus outsourcing it all). Today, when companies want to seize opportunities or avoid problems, IT groups need to figure out how to quickly deliver the systems required to make that happen. If they can't do that—and if all they can do is explain why things can't be done or why things will take 18 months and cost a million dollars—then, as Nicholas Carr suggested, "IT doesn't matter."[7]

The second law states that the best way to be agile is to use simple solutions. Agility requires simplicity because, in order to do things quickly, you need to reduce the number of things that can go wrong. Otherwise, Murphy's Law soon bogs down your best laid but complex plans. How many times have you watched or participated as complex projects struggled, no matter how hard people worked, to overcome one problem after another with no end in sight?

This means practitioners of agile IT learn to size up what, at first, seem to be complex situations. They become skilled at understanding what businesspeople need and they find simple ways to deliver the most important capabilities quickly, often in 30 days or less). Then they stay close to the business as situations unfold and they keep building on the systems they delivered to provide people with new capabilities in a timely manner. Leveraging cloud computing services and SaaS is a highly effective way to do this.

The third law of agility is the law of diminishing returns. It says that doing the same things everybody else is doing is going to yield less and less benefit as time goes on. This law greatly impacts where agility can best be applied. Doing the same old things in an agile way will not provide nearly as much value as applying agility to accomplish brand new things.

This law rewards businesspeople who see new opportunities, and it rewards IT people who find new—yet still simple—ways to deliver what the businesspeople need in order to exploit those opportunities. Where other companies and IT groups use complex and expensive technology, the practitioner of agile IT doesn't always follow the crowd and their "best practices." Practitioners of agile IT aren't afraid to question conventional wisdom and try different approaches.

So, the next time people question whether your company really needs to be agile, ask them how they plan to respond to the law of probability. The next time people downplay your simple IT solutions and instead propose complex systems, ask them how they'll cope with Murphy's Law. And when experts tell you their best practices are the way you should be doing things, ask them how that will help you deal with the law of diminishing returns.

The Consumerization of IT and the Emergence of Cloud-Based, Consumer IT Services

In many companies, there is a standing joke that businesspeople never have to ask IT how long something will take and what it will cost because they already know the answers: It always takes a year and costs a million dollars, and that's just for the simple stuff.

But the days of IT taking forever and projects costing an arm and a leg are clearly coming to an end. The world moves too fast, loans to finance expensive technology projects are harder to get, and some companies are now realizing they have choices other than the traditional solutions of the past 20 years.

People have discovered that, for a growing number of applications, consumer IT is better than corporate IT. It has the features people want, it's more responsive to changing needs, and new features are being added all the time. Consumer IT is often easier to use, faster to install, and a whole lot cheaper to operate. We're talking about things like email and web hosting services from companies like Yahoo and Google, and low-cost or no-cost office productivity, workflow, and collaboration applications provided on a pay-as-you-go, software-as-a-service basis by companies like 37signals, Google, IBM, Twitter, and YouTube, among so many others.

What kinds of business application systems can be built by combining the capabilities of these systems? Companies continue to innovate and create systems that respond to new needs in marketing, sales, customer service, and operations. When speed and simplicity are needed, and there's a desire to explore a new opportunity without committing a lot of money to get started, it makes sense to create systems this way.

For instance, a system to design and launch a new product offering can be developed by combining the collaboration features of Google Apps with the videoconferencing of Skype, and the project management and customer contact management capabilities of 37signals, together with accounting and financials from Workday. This kind of system would be accessed through a web browser. It would have a single logon, and wouldn't require users to switch from one underlying system to another. It would have small chunks of custom code written to tie all these pieces together and move data between the different parts of the system. These systems are known as "mashups." They're quick to build, inexpensive to operate, they can scale up if the business takes off, or they can easily be shut down with no further expense if they are no longer needed.

Using this approach, companies can altogether avoid large capital expenses and instead purchase larger and larger portions of their IT infrastructure as cloud-based services. The spread of high-speed broadband networks and wireless broadband is now making it practical to locate systems infrastructure in the cloud while still delivering fast response times to users across vast geographies.

The Recovering Complexaholic

At times, managers of in-house IT groups or other operating units may object to using consumer IT applications to solve business problems. And sometimes there are legitimate reasons to avoid these products. But it's important to look at the cause of the objections. Some may say it's not scalable as demand grows or that performance is not reliable or data stored in these systems is not secure, yet these objections are often baseless.

Another unstated, perhaps subconscious objection is that this easy-to-use consumer technology doesn't feed our addiction to complexity and support our need to feel important by building complex systems. That said, people and companies indulging their addiction to complexity are doing so at increasing cost and risk to their ability to compete and succeed in our real time global economy.

Consider this scenario: You are the CIO at GlobalCorp, a rapidly growing company run by some street-smart people with a knack for deal making and spotting opportunities ahead of everyone else. Your company operates in North America, Asia, and Europe, and is expanding into Africa, Australia, and South America. You move into new markets and new countries by buying companies and growing them. You exit markets by selling off business units in those areas.

The chief operating officer and the chief financial officer ask you to prepare a presentation for the CEO and board of directors on how IT can help streamline financial reporting and increase the visibility of operations around the world. Some big deals are pending, and they think IT can make a difference. If you're still feeding an addiction to complexity, a little voice in your head says, "Wow, this isn't a simple project; it'll take more than a year and $1 million. Maybe more like three years and $100 million." But if you're a recovering complexaholic, that little voice will say, "These guys are moving fast; they aren't willing to wait three years. What can we do to meet their needs?"

If you're a complexity addict, you round up a group of the usual suspects and put them to work grinding out a long-range development plan. You set a go-live date that's three years off, and you

figure that, in the meantime, everything will just continue to operate as it always has and people in the operating units will just have
to make do with what they already have.

If you're recovering from this addiction, you bring together a
small team of business and IT people and tell them to cast off all
preconceptions. You give them time frames to start delivering us-
able systems to businesspeople within 30 to 90 days. You tell them
everything is on the table, including things that have more in common with consumer IT than corporate IT. Under your guidance,
they develop a strategy that relies on a collection of readily available
IT components like web portals, dashboards and alerts, instant mes-
saging and email, data warehouses, spreadsheets, software-as-a-
service offerings, and small programs that can be quickly coded,
tested, and put into production.

Obviously, it's clear which kind of business and IT executives
are going to thrive in a company like GlobalCorp, but think about
this: in today's hypercompetitive business environment, isn't the
agility that GlobalCorp displays becoming the norm? And is there
any better way to support this agility than by skillful use of cloud
computing and software-as-a-service technology to support new
business operations?

Notes

1. A few of the companies (and their stock symbols) providing cloud and virtuali-
   zation products and services are: Akamai (AKAM); Amazon.com (AMZN);
   Cisco Systems (CSCO); EMC (EMC); Google (GOOG); Hewlett-Packard
   (HPQ); IBM (IBM); Microsoft (MSFT); Rackspace (RAX); Salesforce.com
   (CRM); and Terremark (TMRK).
2. Irving Wladawsky-Berger, in person interview by the authors, IBM Software
   Group, Somers, New York, December 16, 2009.
3. Peter Fingar, *Dot.Cloud: The 21st Century Business Platform* (Tampa, FL: Megan-
   Kiffer Press, 2008).
4. Peter Fingar, phone interview by authors, December 18, 2009.
5. Diamond Management & Technology Consultants, "Don't Waste a Crisis:
   Emerge a Winner by Applying Lessons from the Last Recession" (2008).
   www.diamondconsultants.com/PublicSite/ideas/perspectives/downloads/
   Diamond Recession Report - Dont Waste a Crisis.pdf.
6. In October 2008 *The Economist* magazine came out with a series of articles on
   cloud computing and its business implications. These articles are available for
   subscribers to *The Economist* or can also be purchased at: www.economist.com/
   surveys/displaystory.cfm?story_id=12411864.
7. Nicholas Carr, "IT Doesn't Matter," *Harvard Business Review*, 81 (May 2003).

CHAPTER

10

Global Implications of the Cloud

"**O**pen your eyes, Pilot. A new world is here." So goes the intro to EVE Onlline, one of a new generation of massively multi-player online games (also called MMOGs). In these online games, players from all over the globe log in to realistic, real-time virtual worlds via the Internet. They learn different roles and skill sets, and come together in self-selecting teams to carry out daring missions in pursuit of common goals. So, how is this any different from the challenges that await us in the global, real-time economy that surrounds us?

Real-Time Global Collaboration

If you're part of the generation just starting out in business, answers to this question probably seem pretty obvious. If you're part of a generation that's been around for a while, the answers might not seem so obvious—at first. If you're in your twenties, you may have a set of skills and behaviors that will become increasingly valuable in business, and you probably developed them through many hours of online gaming. Popular MMOGs like EVE Online,[1] EverQuest,[2] and World of Warcraft[3] bring together hundreds of thousands of simultaneous online players from countries around the world to interact in complex, lifelike, three-dimensional worlds based on themes from *Star Wars* science fiction to *Lord of the Rings* adventure fantasy.

MMOGs are not to be confused with single-person shooter games where individual players steal cars, blast aliens and tough guys, and get into street fights. Those games develop fast hand-eye coordination, but not much in the way of business skills. And we aren't talking about virtual social worlds like Second Life either.

Simulation Games Teach Skills

What we're talking about is online games where there are rules and politics and opportunities to collaborate with others and build your reputation and your fortune. To succeed in these games, players have to interact with each other and build relationships and put together plans and go on missions. They join guilds or corporations operated in these games. They develop specific skills related to the roles they play, like pilot, trader, wizard, warrior, hunter, and priest, and they develop reputations and rating levels based on their successes and failures.

The potential for using MMOGs to develop skills that people need to succeed in the global economy is getting serious attention. Recently, a study titled "Virtual Worlds, Real Leaders" was conducted by IBM in conjunction with professors from Stanford University and MIT. They focused their study on the MMOG called World of Warcraft, known as WoW by gamers, and here's some of what they found (this study was conducted in 2008):

There are currently about 73 million online gamers worldwide with a compound annual growth rate of 36.5 percent. The average age of online gamers is 35 years; and 56 percent are male and 44 percent are female. Other findings revolve around leadership responsiveness concepts, and specifically, their findings point out the differences in how those concepts are practiced in MMOGs and in the traditional corporate world.

Leadership in the Old World and the New

We've grown accustomed to leadership in the corporate world being restricted to a relatively small group of people who are identified, mentored, and promoted by the company's senior management. In contrast, leadership in the MMOG world is distributed over a wide group of people who work to increase their own skill levels and who are promoted by consensus within the groups in which they operate.

In the corporate world, as the saying goes, it's often not what you know but who you know. In other words, people get a chance for leadership only if they are noticed by senior management. How many subordinates can a senior manager really notice? (And how much dysfunctional, brown-nosing behavior is motivated by the urgent desire of subordinates to be noticed?) Since senior management is always only a small number of people, the total number of people in a company who can ever be noticed and get a chance to lead is also small, so plenty of qualified people never get a chance.

In MMOGs, the players' skills and aptitudes are constantly measured and made transparently clear to everyone. All players can see the skill levels and success rates of all the other players interacting. Because everyone can see everyone else's qualifications for leadership, the number of people who can become leaders is large. All qualified people get noticed.

Serious Games

Certain types of games can be seen as a form of simulation modeling, and simulation games are a useful way to explore situations that are composed of many actors in situations where they are not linked together in clear cause-and-effect chains of action and reaction. For example, there's no need to use gaming to simulate how a group of billiard balls will move around a table when other billiard balls are shot into their midst. Although there are many actors in this situation, their interactions are well defined in a clear set of cause-and-effect sequences. But gaming is an effective way to simulate how a group of companies working on a project together might behave under different circumstances. The interactions between the actors in this situation are not a clear set of cause-and-effect actions and reactions.

To simulate such a situation, we can define a set of rules that identify the different types of actors involved, the capabilities of each actor, and the different actions each actor can perform. These rules and actors can then be combined in the form of a game where the object of the game is for actors to accomplish certain goals. These are called "serious games."[4]

Serious games have been used for decades by military organizations around the world to simulate how opponents might attack—and how to best counter and reverse the attacks. The outcome of repeated simulations using serious games is often the basis for military strategy and policy. Today, serious games are finding applications in business environments, and some companies are starting to use them to simulate complex business situations and to find effective responses to challenges and opportunities that emerge.

A Supply Chain Game

For example, consider what could happen if a serious game was applied to simulate and optimize the operation of a complex business network like a global supply chain. This is a game that has some pretty stringent rules. Players need to figure out how to deliver products where and when they are needed to meet demand, while at the same time minimizing inventory levels and holding down transportation and manufacturing costs. If you succeed in keeping down inventory levels and costs, but fail to meet product demand, you lose. If you always deliver the products, but fail to keep the other factors under control, then your costs get out of hand and you don't make any money.

How do people and companies learn to excel in this kind of business? In the old days, it was trial and error, making mistakes, and hoping to learn fast enough so that you didn't go out of business before you got better at it. But the learning curve is much steeper now. The rising costs of fuel oil and other commodities are forcing companies around the world to rethink and redesign the supply chains they've built over the last 25 years. Supply chains will need to continually adjust as prices and other factors change. With profit margins so thin, and conditions changing so quickly, it's getting risky to learn by trial and error alone.

Suppose the simulation game provided a map, and on it companies working together in a supply chain could draw in their factories, warehouses, retail stores, and draw in the transportation routes like roads, railways, and harbors that connect those locations. Figure 10.1 is a conceptual diagram of this idea. Then, suppose companies could also define the production volumes of the factories, storage capacity of the warehouses, and movement capacity of the different modes of transportation. Finally, suppose they could associate operating costs with each facility and each mode of transportation.

As the players in this game collaborate to design effective supply chains to respond to changing conditions, the system would constantly keep track of the operating characteristics of the supply chains created, and the players could select the designs that provided the best results. Once that supply chain was in operation, the

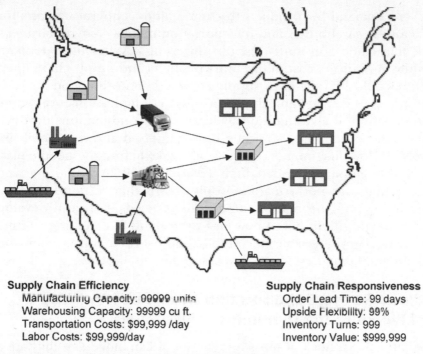

Supply Chain Efficiency
Manufacturing Capacity: 09999 units
Warehousing Capacity: 99999 cu ft.
Transportation Costs: $99,999 /day
Labor Costs: $99,999/day

Supply Chain Responsiveness
Order Lead Time: 99 days
Upside Flexibility: 99%
Inventory Turns: 999
Inventory Value: $999,999

Figure 10.1   A Real-Time Supply Chain Game

system would collect live data feeds from the actual facilities and parties in the supply chain and display the real-time status of ongoing operations. All of this would be hosted in the cloud and it would always be on and available. It would be a massively multiplayer online game, and the object would be for its players to monitor and manage their supply chains in order to best respond to changing business conditions.

Games Support Collaborative Decision Making

Then, imagine a real-time flow of data that showed the inventory levels on hand at each location and in transit along with forecasted product demand at each of the retail stores. Now you have a serious game. The simulation gaming software allows people to try different combinations of factories and warehouses and transportation modes for different products. People can see if a given combination will deliver enough products to the retail stores to meet projected demand. And they can see the operating costs associated with each combination.

As demand for products fluctuates, and as operating costs for factories, warehouses, and transportation modes change, business-people could constantly test out different ways to meet demand while minimizing cost. If inventory planners and supply chain operators could literally draw supply chain configurations on an electronic map display, and then run those configurations over some time period, they would quickly learn what combinations produce the best results. They would become immersed and completely involved. Now imagine how long it would take before the people playing this game developed high levels of skill in designing and operating high-performance supply chains that responded effectively to changing market conditions. They'd learn and develop accurate intuitions about how best to respond to changing circumstances. They'd be able to constantly adjust their supply chains to maintain the highest service levels at the lowest costs.

Cloud-Based Collaboration Enables a New Way of Working: The Dynamics of Swarming

What makes a flock of birds or a school of fish move as if they are a single entity? What makes them all suddenly rise, turn, and accelerate at the same time? There's something else at work here besides just a leader bird or a captain fish telling all the others what to do. This quick, coordinated behavior from large groups of individuals is called swarming. What can we learn from the dynamics of swarming that's relevant to the way we structure and operate businesses in our real-time economy?

Swarms place more emphasis on decentralized coordination, rather than on centralized control, to get things done. We are used to the hierarchical, top-down model of centralized command and control, but this model is proving too rigid, too slow moving, too cumbersome to deliver the responsiveness we need. How can we use the quick coordination we see in swarms to guide our companies?

One way is to use a business model where senior managers tell their people *what* their objectives are, but then let people figure out *how* they will achieve those objectives. In this model, people need to learn how their individual actions combine to create larger effects within the company to move it toward achieving senior management's objectives, even as situations continue to change in unpredictable ways.

Business process management (BPM) and complex event processing (CEP) systems are key components of any business model that emphasizes this kind of decentralized coordination. These systems provide the real-time monitoring and display of operating results that people need to make business progress. When everyone knows their objectives or performance targets, when they can see moment to moment what is going on and whether operations in their areas are on target or off target, then the swarming dynamic starts to engage.

A notion like swarming behavior violates our classic concepts of command and control, and it sounds pretty chaotic. We might agree that swarming behavior could work when objectives are simple and short term, but for more complex and longer-term objectives, our tendency is to think that we need complex management and control procedures. And it seems like decentralization of control is neither time nor resource efficient because the number of technical and performance issues is so large and their interdependencies are so difficult to unravel.

New Ideas Often Seem Counterintuitive at First

Let's look at this more closely by using a historical analogy. The great economic debate of the twentieth century was the rivalry between countries that believed the best way to operate was with a centrally planned economy versus those that believed the free-market was the best. One group held that a centrally controlled, rationally organized economy that was directed by experts was the best way to deal with all of the complex issues that would arise. The other group said all that was needed was enforcement of a reasonable and prudent set of regulations including respect for contracts, honest and transparent reporting of financial results, and prohibitions against excessive and irresponsible risk taking. Once those regulations were in place, people and companies could effectively organize and control themselves on their own without further intervention.

To illustrate the counterintuitive nature of this debate, imagine that a high-level delegation from the government of a developing nation was trying to figure out which of these two models to adopt. First, they visited the trading floor of a stock exchange in a free-market country. What they saw was a chaotic crowd scene. People were running about writing things on scraps of paper. They were shouting at each other, waving their arms, making hand signals. And the walls were covered with huge computer screens and electronic displays showing a constantly changing barrage of numbers and words.

Then the delegation visited the ministry of economic planning in a country using a centrally planned economy. They saw buildings filled with rows of orderly desks. Well-educated scientists, engineers, and economists collected information. And the ministry made plans and issued orders for what each sector of the economy should produce and when and how much would be needed in order to meet the nation's economic goals. Which model do you think the delegation recommended to their government when they returned home from their travels? And yet by the end of the twentieth century, which model proved to be the more efficient?

Most companies still use traditional hierarchical organization models and employ centralized command and control methods. These companies focus on the traditional industrial concepts of economies of scale and achieving high productivity through rigorous application of standard operating procedures. Most employees of these companies have their work closely regulated by supervisors and bosses. There is little incentive for anyone except senior managers in these companies to take any initiative or to try anything different from the norm. This model works well enough in low-change and predictable markets, but those kinds of markets aren't common anymore.

The notion that a central person or group can do all the thinking for everybody else and tell them what to do and when to do it—no matter how many fancy computer systems they may have—is fundamentally flawed. No amount of centralized reporting systems and computing power can adequately deal with the amount of data that needs to be processed in the short time frames business requires today. The answer lies in breaking up the data to be processed, and the decisions to be made, into many smaller jobs that can all be run simultaneously. This is swarming dynamics. It is similar to the concept used in the design of massively parallel computer networks like the Internet itself.

Decentralized Coordination Replaces Centralized Control

Companies that employ decentralized control structures that incentivize and train their people to think and act for themselves, and provide them with the real-time performance data they need to make good decisions, will outperform their competitors. Very simply, this is because people working in self-directed teams striving to achieve common performance objectives can find hundreds of ways to make small, continuous adjustments that will increase their profits and decrease their costs every day, every week, every month.

These companies benefit from a continuous stream of efficiencies generated by many small, rapid adjustments as business situations change. They also benefit from profits gained by quickly responding to market opportunities as they appear.

Walk through any company. Talk to people in the operating units. Ask them if they know ways to make their activities more productive and ways to save more money. Ask them if they know ways to better serve customers and if they have ideas for new products or services that customers might want. In most cases people will answer yes to all these questions.

What would happen if senior managers gave people clear performance objectives and then got out of the way? What would happen if people received a constant stream of performance data from BPM and CEP systems that showed them the results of their actions and if they were effective or not? People would see if they were on track to achieve their objectives and they could respond by getting back on track when things went wrong.

How fast would people learn to act on their own initiative and be more productive, save money, increase customer service, and offer new products and services? Would they soon learn to regularly meet or exceed the performance objectives they were given?

Swarming behavior causes an organization to act as a single coordinated entity. An apt analogy for this is the human body. It can be seen as a swarm of cells that continually sense their environment and act on their own without waiting to be told what to do. Our brains are not aware of everything that our bodies are doing nor do they need to be. Individual cells and organs know how to act on their own. And the overall effect of these swarming cells is to produce the coordinated behavior that makes our lives possible.

Unlike the slower and more predictable industrial economy of the twentieth century, we live in an unpredictable global economy and the best efficiencies come from swarming dynamics that make hundreds of small adjustments to respond quickly as situations change. Organizations operating like this are structured as networks of many self-directed operating units that respond quickly without waiting to be told what to do.

Cloud-based BPM and CEP systems provide the people in these operating units with the real-time information they need. People know what their performance objectives are, and they have the training and authority need to act effectively. This is a powerful way to operate in high-change environments.

It is a mistake to use BPM and CEP systems to merely strengthen traditional centralized command and control procedures. That usually produces the opposite of the desired effect, just as centrally planned economies actually produced less efficiency and productivity, not more. The real power of these systems lies in driving the organizational swarming of self-directed operating units. They can enable people to monitor operations and learn to make their own decisions—just as individual companies act in a free market and just as cells act in our bodies.

Real-Time Visibility Could Make Us a Whole Lot Smarter

The dynamics of swarming scale up from individual companies to entire industry value chains and trading networks. Consider what could happen if we were to apply cloud-based systems to provide real-time visibility into global ecosystems and allow people anywhere in the world to access and act on that visibility.

If we could see our world as it changes, would that set up a powerful feedback loop enabling us to learn to respond effectively to those changes? Perhaps the best way to learn to live in balance with our planet and the interdependent ecosystems that support our life is to make those ecosystems visible. Seeing is believing. If all of us (not just select groups of experts) can see what's happening as it happens, then maybe we can all figure out what we need to do to.

Traditional approaches to managing our environment call for selected groups of experts to collect reams of data and publish their findings and recommendations in lengthy reports that are then used (in greater or lesser degrees) to formulate rules and regulations to control the behavior of the rest of us. A new approach is to build networks of environmental sensors and combine the data streams coming from those sensors into real-time displays that show everyone what's happening, so all of us can participate in deciding

Figure 10.2   Galway Bay on the West Coast of Ireland

what needs to be done. We wonder which approach will prove to be more effective.

The Irish government is experimenting with this new approach in a project intended to better understand and manage the ecosystem and natural resources of Galway Bay on the west coast of Ireland (see Figure 10.2).

The Ireland Marine Institute has partnered with IBM to deploy a network of sensors for monitoring conditions in the bay. This is the first phase in the creation of the SmartBay Environmental Monitoring System and it is now sending real-time data back to the Marine Institute, where it is used to create real-time dashboards and maps for use by different constituencies—fishermen, tourists, ship captains, government agencies, and the like—to enable them to respond appropriately as conditions change. This project is a glimpse of how humans can learn how to live in balance with our world.

Technology Used and What the Sensor Network Measures

The Ireland Marine Institute worked with IBM to design and deploy a network of sensors tied to buoys that were deployed in Galway Bay in the summer of 2009. The sensor buoys were built by the Dublin-based company TechWorks Marine. Figure 10.3 is a picture from the Marine Institute website that shows what the sensor buoys look like.

Each SmartBay buoy supports an array of advanced ocean sensors that collect and transmit real-time information on ocean conditions that benefit scientists, commercial fishermen, fish farmers,

Figure 10.3   Galway Bay Sensor Buoys

Photos courtesy of Ireland Marine Institute—photo on left by Phil Trickett.

environmental monitoring agencies, and the general public. The buoys transmit their data to the Marine Institute via a wireless WiMAX network, where it is displayed through a web portal showing the real-time conditions in the bay. The different constituencies of people using this portal can easily access the data of most interest to them.

The sensors on the buoys are loaded with IBM software, and new versions can be remotely downloaded as needed via WiMAX. At present, the sensors are measuring environmental conditions in the bay like air and sea temperature, wind velocity, rainfall, currents and tides, wave action, and chemical makeup of the seawater. Figure 10.4 shows a screenshot of the SmartBay portal. The Galway Bay project is a prototype example of what a cloud-based environmental sensor network could look like.

How a Smart Species Can Get Smarter

So far, we humans are the most successful species on this planet, and our success is a testament to how smart we are. Over the past couple of centuries, we've learned how to employ industrial technology to efficiently extract and process our planet's resources so that we can improve our standard of living. Now we need to get even smarter and learn how to use information technology to continue that improvement, while at the same time, finding ways to live within limits that our planet's ecosystems can sustain over the long haul. That's going to be tricky.

We're an argumentative species and we don't like others telling us what to do. It's hard to comprehend the changes brought

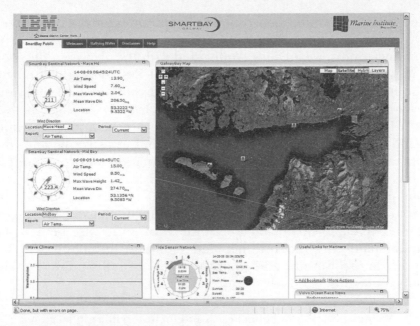

Figure 10.4   Galway SmartBay Portal

Screenshot courtesy of Ireland Marine Institute and IBM.

about by our growing population and our growing use of natural resources. Many of us still remember a time when this planet seemed infinite in resources, and it's hard to confront the notion that there actually are limits. We all have to be involved in figuring out how to live in balance with Mother Earth because, if we leave the job to select groups of experts and regulators, the rest of us won't believe what they tell us, and we won't accept the regulations they propose.

So clearly, seeing is believing. Real-time visibility and transparency is the best way to promote efficient markets in finance and commerce. It's the best way to promote good government, and it's the best way to deal with the tough choices and lifestyle changes we need to make in this century.

New Realities and New Opportunities

In his book *The Empathic Civilization,* Jeremy Rifkin presents a vision of how the global spread of real-time (or near-real-time) technology like the Internet, social media, mobile computing, and the cloud is promoting a growing sense of the relationships and interconnections between people and our planet's biosphere. He points out that, along with the growth of this new sense of connectedness, we are also confronted with the growing effects of widespread pollution and environmental destruction caused by the industrial technology that supported our standard of living over the past 100 years.

He makes a compelling case that we are in a race, on one hand, between approaching environmental catastrophe and, on the other hand, learning to harness information and communications technology to support new ways of living in balance with our planet's ecosystem. Rifkin suggests that we need to see the rapid growth of the Internet and related technology in the larger context created by this race because it will otherwise be hard to understand why the Internet and cloud technology could be spreading so rapidly, and what their real benefits might be. He puts it like this:

> We talk breathlessly about access and inclusion in a global communications network, but speak little of exactly why we want to communicate with one another on such a planetary scale. What's sorely missing is an overarching reason for why billions of human beings should be increasingly connected. Toward what end? The only feeble explanations thus far offered are to share information, be entertained, advance commercial exchange, and speed the globalization of the economy. All the above, while relevant, nonetheless seem insufficient to justify why nearly seven billion human beings should be connected and mutually embedded in a globalized society. Seven billion individual connections, absent any overall unifying purpose, seem a colossal waste of human energy.[5]

His line of reasoning about the overarching purpose of all this technology leads to some obvious and profound questions. For instance, what if the universal, real-time visibility made possible by this technology caused countries to see continuing environmental deterioration and its attendant dangers of ecological collapse as one of the largest and most imminent threats they face? What if countries started spending to protect themselves against this new threat the same way they spend on protecting themselves against traditional military threats?

What if governments began redirecting portions of their military budgets to address this new threat? Would the environmental sensor business and related lines of environmental monitoring and remediation be a good industry for companies to enter? The global infrastructure for this business is cloud computing, and that infrastructure is being rolled out at an accelerating pace as you read these words.

The growing, worldwide, cloud computing infrastructure is supporting the creation of many new companies that are developing software and devices for application systems to address unique industry needs in ways never before possible. These companies no longer need to spend money on building data centers to host their software-as-a-service offerings and support their internal operations. They can instead devote their resources to optimizing and enhancing their customer-facing applications. In addition, they can use web search engines like Google, Yahoo, Bing, and Ask (these are the new global yellow pages) to develop more efficient ways to attract customers. Increasingly, customers find these new companies by conducting keyword searches or by hearing about them through social media. Companies can find new customers and close business deals without the labor-intensive sales processes of the past. This is why the cloud is so important; it is changing the business ecosystem, and it has the potential to also change the world's ecosystem.

Rifkin offers this opinion of how the global network of information and communication technology can be harnessed to address our energy needs:

> "It was the first Industrial Revolution that brought together print and literacy with coal steam and rail. The second combined the telegraph and telephone with the internal combustion engine and oil. What we now have now is the possibility of a distributed energy revolution. We can all create our own energy, store it, and then distribute it to each other. Twenty-five years from now, millions of buildings will become power plants that will load renewable energy. We will load solar power from the sun, wind from turbines, and even ocean waves on each coast. We can also make the power grid of the world smart and intelligent; we call it inter-grid. Not far from now, millions and millions of people will load power to buildings, store it in

the form of hydrogen and distribute energy peer-to-peer; just like digital media and the internet."[6]

The power generation model that supports our civilization will change with the spread of smart power grids that are based on the universal flow of real-time information. The cloud will enable creation of tens of thousands of new businesses to deliver whole new categories of products and services to bring smart power grids to every part of the world.

Power generation will return once again to individual home and office buildings, but it will be a far cry from the wood burning, coal fired, or fuel oil–based technology that once powered individual buildings. It will be sustainable and it will tap the energy of sun, wind, and waves. It will work over regional networks composed of central power stations and thousands or millions of individual, interconnected power consumers and generators. When extra power is needed by individuals, they will draw it from the network; and when they are generating more power than they need, they will send their excess power back to the network to be allocated to where it is needed.

And this brings us back to our original analogy for cloud computing in Chapter 1. We said that traditional in-house IT infrastructure is going to be outsourced to cloud vendors who enjoy economies of scale and thus offer computing services at lower and lower price points. This is clearly happening.

Yet there's another trend happening that we discussed in Chapters 7 and 8: the trend of embedding new, innovative IT systems and IT professionals ever more deeply into the very business units that at the same time are outsourcing the operation and ownership of their traditional information and communications technology.

Racing toward Global Awareness: The One

Cisco's Visual Networking Index: Global Mobile Data Traffic Forecast Update, 2009–2014, states that, "Global mobile traffic will double every year through 2014, increasing 39 times between 2009 and 2014. Mobile data traffic will grow at a compound annual growth rate (CAGR) of 108 percent between 2009 and 2014, reaching 3.6 exabytes per month by 2014."[7] (An exabyte is one billion gigabytes.)

Furthermore, by 2014, about 66 percent of the world's mobile data traffic will be video, and mobile video will grow at a CAGR of 131 percent between 2009 and 2014. Mobile video has the highest growth rate of any application category measured within the forecast. The Middle East and Africa are projected to have the highest growth rate of any region at 133 percent CAGR, followed by Asia Pacific at 119 percent and North America at 117 percent.

The study shows that audio communications will be dwarfed by data and video communications and 66 percent of the world's mobile traffic will be video by 2014. That's a huge change in a very short time. Global mobile traffic will exceed two exabytes per month by 2013 and, regardless of our present economic troubles, it will reach one exabyte per month in half the time previously taken by fixed data traffic.

Mobile devices increase people's individual contact time with the network. Mobile voice service is already considered a necessity by many, and mobile data, video, and TV services are now also becoming an essential part of people's lives. In addition, mobile machine-to-machine (M2M) connections continue to increase. The coming years will see constantly increasing adoption of mobile video despite economic conditions.

What could all this mean? It's as if our planet is employing us to build out a nervous system that covers the planet and allows for all of us to plug into it and see what is happening, as it happens.

Similar to Human Development

This growth of global communications and computing networks is somewhat analogous to our own progress. We humans emerged as the creatures we are today when our cerebral cortex blossomed within our developing brain. In that expansion of the cerebral cortex, we awoke and became aware of ourselves. Our planet (Mother Earth) has spawned this whole unruly lot of us, and now perhaps she is using us to grow a network over the top of us that encompasses all geographical points on her surface. And in the expansion of this global network—this planetary cerebral cortex—there might emerge a new awareness.

Kevin Kelly is a noted commentator, journalist, and thought leader on the impact of digital technology on society and individuals. He was a founding editor of Wired magazine and has contributed work to publications including *The Economist, Time, Harper's Magazine, Science,* and the *New York Times.* His book *Out of Control: The New Biology of Machines, Social Systems, and the Economic World*[8] delivers insights into the workings of complex organizations and organisms. He builds on the themes of cybernetics and general systems theory and shows findings from several fields of contemporary science and philosophy that illustrate how intelligence is not organized as a centralized function, but instead is organized as a network or a swarm like a hive of bees.

He made an insightful presentation in 2007 titled "Predicting the Next 5,000 Days of the Web" at the annual conference of a not-for-profit foundation called TED (Technology, Entertainment, Design). In it, he talks of the phenomenal growth rate the web is experiencing and speculates on where it's taking us. He ends his presentation with the thought that all this growth is leading to the creation of what we call the cloud, or what he calls the "One," and he describes it like this (note that OS stands for operating system):

> There is only one machine.
> The web is its OS.
> All screens look into the One.
> No bits will live outside the web.
> To share is to gain.
> Let the One read it.
> The One is us.[9]

Notes

1. EVE Online is a game based on a *Star Wars*-type theme, www.eveonline.com/.
2. EverQuest is based on a dungeons and dragons theme, http://everquest.station.sony.com/.
3. World of Warcraft is based on a *Lord of the Rings*-type of theme, www.worldof-warcraft.com/index.xml.
4. Serious games are used extensively in the military and health care for training of soldiers and health care delivery professionals. Many universities are also using serious games for educational purposes. And now serious games are also being used as a collaboration platform. The Wikipedia listing for serious games is a good place to start a larger investigation of serious games and their evolving uses; http://en.wikipedia.org/wiki/Serious_game.
5. Jeremy Rifkin, *The Empathic Civilization: The Race to Global Consciousness in a World in Crisis* (New York: Tarcher/Penguin, 2010), p. 594.
6. Ibid, p. 517.

7. Cisco Systems Inc., "Cisco Visual Networking Index: Global Mobile Data Traffic Forecast Update, 2009–2014," paper (February 9, 2010), www.cisco .com/en/US/solutions/collateral/ns341/ns525/ns537/ns705/ns827/white_ paper_c11-520862.html.
8. Kevin Kelly, *Out of Control: The New Biology of Machines, Social Systems, and the Economic World* (New York: Basic Books, 1995) [orig. pub. 1992].
9. Kevin Kelly, "The Next 5,000 Days of the Web," presentation at TED conference (filmed December 2007), www.ted.com/index.php/talks/kevin_ kelly_on_the_next_5_000_days_of_the_web.html.

About the Authors

Michael Hugos, principal at Center for Systems Innovation [c4si], delivers seminars and briefings on strategies for business and IT agility and mentors teams in agile systems development. He previously spent six years as chief information officer (CIO) of a multibillion dollar distribution co-operative where he developed the suite of supply chain and e-business systems that transformed the company's operations and revenue model. He is a recognized expert in agility and supply chain management. He won the CIO 100 Award in 2003 and 2005 for bold and resourceful use of technology, the InformationWeek 500 Award in 2005 for innovative use of technology in wholesale distribution, and in 2006 he was selected for the Computerworld Premier 100 Award for career achievement.

Michael earned his MBA from Northwestern University's Kellogg School of Management and holds an undergraduate degree in Urban Planning and Design from the University of Cincinnati. He writes a blog for *CIO* magazine titled "Doing Business in Real Time" and he has authored several books in addition to this one including *Business Agility: Sustainable Prosperity in a Relentlessly Competitive World*, and the popular *Essentials of Supply Chain Management*, now going into its third edition. He can be reached via his web site at. www .MichaelHugos.com.

Derek Hulitzky, Vice President of Content Development at a global technology media company, is a keen industry watcher with an intense focus on how CIOs and companies manage their technology teams and responsibilities. A seasoned technology marketer, he is an accomplished business and technology panel and event moderator with a rich background in technology content creation, audience development, and management. He holds a Bachelor of Science degree from the Whittemore School of Business and Economics at the University of New Hampshire, and an MBA from Bentley University.

Index